Starlight City

'Where?' I asked. 'Where will you go?'
'The City,' she said.
'The City! Have you got any idea what it's like there?
You won't last five minutes.'

It is the year 2050. When Kari's mother brings home a weird old woman she finds wandering in the road, Kari is appalled. What could have possessed her mother to pick up a scruffy old Misfit—or even a Drifter?

But Kari soon realizes there is more to Rachel than she first thought. There is something about her—her soft voice, her gentle aura, her love of music—which wins Kari over. So when the police arrive, looking for Rachel, and take her away for questioning, Kari decides she must go to the City and look for her, not realizing that this is just the beginning of an adventure that will change her life . . .

SUE WELFORD was born in Sussex and trained to be a secretary before giving up paid work to bring up her children. When they started school, she had several part-time jobs, and then became an editorial writer with a local newspaper. When she was made redundant, she continued writing at home and had several articles published in magazines. After five rejected novels, her first book for young adults was published in 1989. *Starlight City* is the seventh of her books to be published by Oxford University Press.

Starlight City

Other books by Sue Welford

Ghost in the Mirror
Snowbird Winter
Charlie in the Pink
Charlie on the Spot
The Night After Tomorrow
The Shadow of August

Starlight City

Sue Welford

Oxford University Press

Oxford New York Toronto

For Diana, Princess of Wales
'You were the wind beneath our wings'.

Oxford University Press, Great Clarendon Street,
Oxford OX2 6DP

Oxford New York
Athens Auckland Bangkok Bogota Bombay
Buenos Aires Calcutta Cape Town Dar es Salaam
Delhi Florence Hong Kong Istanbul Karachi
Kuala Lumpur Madras Madrid Melbourne
Mexico City Nairobi Paris Singapore
Taipei Tokyo Toronto Warsaw

and associated companies in
Berlin Ibadan

Oxford is a trade mark of Oxford University Press

Copyright © Sue Welford 1998
First published 1998

A CIP catalogue record for this book is available
from the British Library

Cover illustration by Rob Hefferan

ISBN 0 19 271791 X

Printed in Great Britain

I am the ghost of Shadwell Stair.
Along the wharves by the water-house,
And through the cavernous slaughter-house
I am the shadow that walks there.

Yet I have flesh both firm and cool,
And eyes tumultuous as the gems
Of moons and lamps in the lapping Thames
When dusk sails wavering down the Pool.

From 'Shadwell Stair' by *Wilfred Owen*

How can you tell the legend from the fact on
these worlds that lie so many years away?
Planets without names, called by their people
simply *The World* . . .

From 'Semley's Necklace'
by *Ursula Le Guin*

PART ONE

In the Country

Last night, I had a really weird dream. There were people coming towards me. Not the tourists that flock here in the vacation weeks but people in strange clothes . . . all walking out of bright sunlight . . . huge figures with hands outstretched. They moved together, like puppets on invisible strings. Vague . . . indistinct . . . as if a heavy mist swirled around them and they were having to push their way through it. It was their eyes that scared me. Staring right at me. Eyes that I couldn't resist.

I woke feeling grey and groggy. The edges of the dream still haunted my mind. Then I remembered what day it was and the illusion flitted away. The first day of the summer holidays. Great!

I hopped out of bed, charged to the window, and opened the shutters. My heart plummeted to the soles of my feet. Rain. Huge oily drops rolling down the glass, quicksilver against the backdrop of leaden skies. I pressed my nose to the pane and watched the grey sheets of water. Everything outside was obscured by a curtain of mist. The garden, the lane, the hills beyond . . . everything.

I could have wept. Jake and I *had* got it all planned. He would come over first thing. We would bike to the terminal and catch the suburban-link tramway. It would take us to Bluelake—the out-of-City complex nearest to us. We could go for a swim at the sports pavilion, mooch along the boulevard, eat in the food hall, listen to whatever rockband was playing in the square, maybe

3

even take in a film at the moviedrome before we got the tram home.

'Chill out, Kari,' Jake said on the videophone when I called him. 'We can go tomorrow.'

'Tomorrow?' I gazed gloomily at the torrent outside. 'It's going to rain for ever.'

Jake had chuckled. 'Are you a meteorologist all of a sudden?'

Only Jake would say meteorologist instead of weather forecaster like any normal person. His brown eyes gazed at me from the screen.

'You can always tell by the way the mist sits on top of the hills,' I said. 'Believe me. I know about these things. I've lived here almost all my life.'

Jake had only come to live along our road a couple of years ago.

I dragged my eyes from his face and looked out at the hills, looming dark and mysterious in the distance. I could see the stark, stone outlines of the long-abandoned railway station brooding just beyond the road. I often tried to imagine what it was like when trains rattled along the rails and commuters seethed their way to and from the City. My brother, Damien, and I used to creep out and play there sometimes until Mum found out and we were forbidden to go there. We used to have a great time. Making camps, having pretend laser fights with broken chair legs, racing up and down the derelict and weed-ridden platforms. Sometimes I thought I could hear the ghost-echo of rattling wheels and an eerie hoot as trains entered the tunnel at the far end and came roaring out towards the station. I imagined the thunderous rhythm of their wheels beating in time with my heart.

The tunnel had been bricked up soon after we came to live here and is so covered with a thick tangle of creepers you hardly know it's there. It makes me shudder to think how dark and damp it must be inside. What ghosts might be haunting it. I imagine creepy-

4

crawlies bumbling around in the foul air and all the flotsam and jetsam of a bygone age littering the floor. Enough to give me nightmares for a week.

And so I spent the morning practising a new melody I'd composed for my flute. Playing a few of my favourite micro-discs, twisting my hair on top of my head trying to create fantastic new styles, browsing the World-web, messing around with my brother's VR helmet. I checked to see if the family's numbers had come up on the daily lotto. Needless to say, they hadn't. Sighing, bored, I scanned details of my holiday project.

Society in the last decade of the Twentieth Century.

I groaned and pulled a face. Couldn't they have found something a bit more exciting for us to write about?

Reluctantly, I surfed through one of the Timescan files.

Then the screen told me an e-memo was waiting. My Link Tutor . . .

Have a great holiday—don't forget to get your project in by September.

Typical, I thought.

I went back to Timescan for a while. There didn't seem to be much else I could do on a day like this. I flitted through all the events that led up to the millennium and was just reading about people claiming to have been abducted by aliens when I noticed there was another message waiting. This time it was my web-friend, Vinny. I spend ages swapping messages with her. Hearing all about her life in the suburbs was much more interesting than twentieth-century boredom.

When I accessed the letter, the mail-man appeared on the screen and read it out to me. Vinny wanted to know what I was up to.

I mailed her back, telling her I wasn't doing anything much. Only getting bored.

By mid-afternoon I was cheesed off again. I'd spent another hour playing my flute and charming the cats into a stupor. That cheered me up for a while. We've got several scruffy looking moggies. Strays who wormed their way into our affections by standing vigil at the back door and refusing to budge until they were fed. Mum said they came from the factory-farm up the road where they were expected to scrape a living from killing vermin.

Then I'd logged on again and scanned twentieth-century environmental awareness, politics, techno-advances, space travel, the endless wars. I left my machine in standby and spent a while lying on my bed fantasizing. Sun-kissed sands, blue waters, heady hazy days walking down flower-strewn lanes with Jake. I decided I must be going mad. Jake wouldn't be seen dead strolling down a flower-strewn lane with me or anyone. Even if there were any.

I was gazing out of the window again, willing the rain to pack up, when a car's headlights shone through the gloom. Mum, back from shopping. The gates swung open and the car came into the drive with a thud as Mum hit the gatepost for the third time that month. She got out, straightened it, then went round to the passenger side. She opened the door. Someone unfolded from the seat. A visitor. Wearing a long coat, a scarf round her head, and clutching a poly-bag in each hand. She stood up straight, looked up, and stared at the Cottage as if she was spellbound by the sight of it. Maybe she had never seen a house like it before. Not that there was really anything extraordinary about an ancient, red-brick railway cottage with a grey roof.

The glass had grown misty with my breathing. I rubbed a hole, just big enough for the stranger's figure to fill it. She looked really odd. Old-fashioned winter clothes, thick trousers, boots. The beginning of summer yet she was dressed for the Arctic.

I drew in my breath. A strange feeling rippled down my spine. The kind of sensation you get when you hear a new melody and you manage to work it out and play it yourself. You feel as if your whole body is making it and not just your fingers and your lungs. You feel more alive than at any other time in your existence. Why I should feel like this at the sight of a weird old woman I had no idea. Jake often said I was a nut-case and sometimes I reckoned he was right.

Mum keyed in the security code and the front door opened. A cat yowled. Ro probably. He's always snoozing by the doorway.

'Kari!' Mum's voice rang up the staircase. 'You up there?'

I went out on to the landing.

'Oh, there you are.' Mum took off her jacket and shook it. Raindrops flew out all over Ro in a shower of crystal. He didn't move. He just went on rubbing himself against the hem of the visitor's coat and mioawing *food, food* at her as if she was a lifelong friend.

Mum's friend was ignoring him. She just stood there, hanging her head, her face shrouded by a tatty mustard-colour scarf. She was clutching on to her bags as if she had the crown jewels inside. Maybe it had been her who nicked them all those years ago? She was hunched up, staring down at her feet as if they were the most fascinating things in the universe.

My nose twitched. I could smell something funny. Something like one of the dead creatures the mogs brought in from time to time. Dark and musty, damp . . . old.

Mum grinned up at me. 'Come down and say "Hi" to Rachel.' She went back outside to unload the shopping.

I went down slowly, step by step. I stared at Rachel. She must have felt me looking because she raised her head. Buried in the folds of her scarf, her eyes narrowed. She was standing in the shadow of the open door and that's really all I could see, just her eyes, a tumultuous blue, staring . . .

At me.

Apprehension wriggled down my spine again. I felt the hairs suddenly stand to attention along my arm. It

7

was then that I remembered my dream and the strange feeling it left me with.

A feeling that something was just beginning . . . something that would change my life for ever.

1

'But, Mum, she really stinks . . . !'

'Shh, she'll hear you.' Mum was unpacking the shopping.

I was helping. Scooting to and fro with packets of pasta, cereal, a couple of bottles of my dad's favourite Chardonnay, vintage 2025, that I shoved in the wine rack behind the door. I'd deactivated Archie, our house-robot. He always puts stuff away in the wrong place.

'I don't care if she does.'

I had managed to get rid of that odd feeling I had when I first saw Rachel. When she'd held out her hand in greeting I had touched it warily, briefly. Scared I might catch something from her. That the skin of my fingers might curl up with some grotty disease.

I flung a packet of spaghetti into the cupboard and slammed the door quickly before it fell out again.

Mum was trying to puzzle out why she had a mega-pack of red kidney beans when there were already three in the cupboard.

'I'm sure I didn't order these.' She frowned. 'I must have clicked on the wrong item. I was only allowed half an hour's parking time so I didn't get a chance to check the bags.'

It was nothing new. Once, she had gone to pick up the shopping and found she'd ordered twenty, one-hundred packs of disposable bath-towels by mistake. The garage was chock-a-block with boxes for months even though she managed to sell some off to her friends. She'd offered them on the Net at a reduced price and managed to get rid of half of them.

She shrugged and put the packet of beans on the bottom shelf. She turned towards me. Our eyes are the same colour, ocean green under a fringe of reddish hair. My mother's cut short and neat, mine long and rebellious falling almost to the base of my spine.

'And I care if Rachel hears you,' she said as if she'd just realized what I'd said about her. 'You'll hurt her feelings.'

She narrowed her eyes so I knew she meant business.

'I didn't know Misfits had feelings,' I remarked.

I knew I was being cruel but truth was the old woman scared me. I hated her coming into our house. She was surrounded by an aura that frightened me. Auras are a kind of haze that surround some people. It's with them wherever they go, changing colour with their mood. Often people don't have to tell me how they're feeling— I can usually see it for myself. I'm the only person I know who can do it. It began when I was about four years old, not long after we moved here. When I told Mum she thought my eyesight had gone wonky. She took me to the medi-centre for an eye scan. They couldn't find anything wrong and to Mum's embarrassment said it was probably a figment of my imagination. They said kids who had a gift for music often had vivid imaginations too. That I would probably grow out of it. I'm still waiting. I don't talk about it much. People only look at me as if I'm potty. When I told Jake, he just gave me a strange look and said I would have been burned as a witch if I'd lived in the olden days.

Rachel's aura puzzled me. It wasn't like anything I'd seen before. It could have been because I'd never *met* a Misfit before. And the truth was I wasn't particularly over the moon about meeting one now.

My mother was still glaring at me. 'Who says she's a Misfit?'

I shrugged. 'It's pretty obvious, isn't it?'

10

I had decided that's definitely what Rachel was. You only had to take one look at her to realize it. She was one of the homeless, wandering vagrants who haunted the streets of the City. How she'd ended up here in the country I had no idea. And *what* had possessed Mum to bring her into the house, I'd never know. She must have had a brainstorm.

'Not necessarily,' Mum was arguing although she didn't have a leg to stand on. 'Anyway, Misfits never come this far from City limits,' she was saying, 'even if they do manage to get through the turnpikes. There's nothing out here for them.'

'Well, this one has,' I said. 'And you've picked her up. You must be bonkers.'

Mum shook her head. 'No, Kari. You're wrong.' She waved her hand in the air when I started to protest. 'Don't ask me how I know. I just do.'

'Well, if she's not a Misfit, what is she then?'

Mum didn't answer straight away. Then she looked at me.

'I don't know,' she said with an odd expression on her face.

Earlier, when Mum introduced me, she had taken the bags from Rachel's fingers and led her into the kitchen. Rachel had stood there without speaking, just staring at her fascinating feet in their holey old boots that looked about a hundred years old.

'Would you like to freshen up?' Mum had said as if a quick lick and a promise would do the trick.

'Freshen up?' Rachel had glanced at me then dropped her eyes as if the sight of me had burned them.

'Yes.' Mum was standing by the cooker, her arms folded, gazing at her with a look of pity on her face. 'The shower room's first on the left.'

I had been slouching against the door frame, as far away from Rachel as possible. Mum got a couple of towels and thrust them into her arms. 'Put them down the chute when you've finished, they'll go for recycling.'

11

Rachel had mumbled something then shambled her way past me, up the stairs and into the shower room.

'Take Rachel's things up for her,' Mum told me. 'Put them in the spare room.'

'Who . . . me?' I had cringed at the thought of picking up the bags.

'Yes, you.' Mum glared at me. Then she went to the foot of the stairs and called, 'Help yourself to anything you want and take as long as you like. We don't eat until about seven.'

'Thank you,' Rachel called.

As I dumped the bags on the bed I had suddenly been overcome by a kind of morbid curiosity. I wanted to peep inside to see what she had been clutching so jealously. I can't help being nosy, it's just the way I'm made. Under that coat and scarf, you just couldn't tell how old she was, what her hair was like . . . anything. You couldn't see if she was old or young, dark or fair, ugly or pretty. One thing you could tell—she certainly needed to do more than *freshen up*. She was probably infested with parasites. I just hadn't been able to believe Mum was treating her as if she was the President herself.

Rachel had been on the landing, looking round, at the pictures on the walls, the books in the bookcase, the piano, the light from the stained-glass window above the staircase. Her eyes had lingered on each one as if she was hungry for the sight of something beautiful. I hadn't been able to help being suspicious. I'm a great one for making snap judgements but I'd got a horrible feeling she was sussing things out. Trying to decide what was worth the most so she could steal it for booze or drugs money.

I really didn't think I could bear it. A smelly old Misfit in our house, eyeing our things. It really gave me the creeps.

I hadn't had a chance to look in her bags because she had suddenly appeared in the doorway to ask me how to

12

work the shower. I'd shown her, then run back downstairs.

I could hear Rachel now. The loo being flushed, the hiss of the jet-shower, the body-drier humming away merrily. Footsteps shuffling to and fro. Mum had reactivated Archie and he was hovering around the foot of the stairs waiting to go and clean up after her.

'Anyway,' I said to Mum when we'd finished putting away the shopping. 'Where did you find her?'

'She found me really,' Mum explained. 'I stopped the car to watch a blackbird. I haven't seen one for years. And suddenly there she was, trudging along the road. I offered her a lift but she didn't seem to have any idea where she wanted to go. She was cold and wet and confused so I brought her here.'

'Why didn't you just give her some money and drive on? That's what anyone with any sense would have done.'

'I tried . . . she wouldn't take it. She just looked at it then shook her head.'

'Honestly, Mum,' I scoffed. 'She's conning you. Most Misfits would kill for a few Euros. She'll probably pinch something valuable then disappear. These people only—'

Then Mum did something that really surprised me. She came right up to me and got hold of my arm. Hard. Digging her nails through the sleeve of my sportsuit top. For someone who insists she never uses violence against her children she was squeezing really viciously.

'Is it too much to ask that you actually think of someone else other than yourself for a change?' She gave me a real piranha look and her eyes spiralled green lights of anger at me.

'OK, OK, I apologize,' I said hastily, although I wasn't a bit sorry.

I plonked down at the table. Sulking. I felt decidedly grey and gloomy. I leant my chin on my hands and stared out at the rain. The bad weather was an omen. It was going to last all summer. For one thing, there wouldn't be any tourists coming to gawk at our house. I really enjoy watching from the garden while the old rail enthusiasts cruise past staring at us as if we're monkeys in a safari park. I know they envy us our fresh air and green fields and cute little cottage even if the trains are long gone.

My mum was right, though. I *was* being totally selfish about Rachel but there is a limit to how sympathetic a person can be.

'I just think you're mad, that's all,' I told Mum, wanting the last word as usual. 'These people—'

She turned in a red fury, angrier than I'd ever seen her before.

'These people? What do you know about *these people*? You live away from the City and you've got a loving family. You're in a cocoon, Kari. It's about time you started to grow up and realize there are other people in the World besides yourself. People less fortunate.' Her voice shook.

I rolled my eyes. Mum is always going on about how fortunate we are. She's like a jingle you keep hearing then you can't get it off your brain. I *know* we're fortunate. Fortunate that is if you like living in a place with no street lights, no close neighbours, no stores, no games-arcades, no moviedomes, and the minimum of pollution. Mum doesn't have to keep on about it. That was exactly *why* a smelly old Misfit from goodness-knows-where scared me so much.

'Well, Dad's going to go ballistic.' I hoped the thought of my father's wrath might change her mind. I should have known better.

'He can say what he likes,' she said. 'Rachel is my guest.'

'Guest!'

I got up. My chair fell with a crack on the floor. Mum had spoilt everything with one of her crazy do-gooding ideas. How could I ask my Net-friends to visit with Rachel here? I could just imagine Emma or Vinny turning up and that horrible old woman shambling around in old rags and stinking like a trashcan. I would just simply die.

'Well, don't expect *me* to sit at the dinner table with her, will you!' I shouted. 'I'll throw up!'

I knew I was behaving like a spoilt brat but I couldn't help it.

I flung through the door and almost tripped over Ro washing himself in the doorway.

'Bloody cat!' I shouted.

Two hands scooped him up out of my way. The deep, brown voice murmured, 'Poor puss, you almost squashed him.'

Long fingers stroked his inky fur, caressing him, soothing him. He purred, a soft rumbling like the echo of a terrorist bomb blast. He rubbed his face traitorously against her arm. Old Ro was usually a pretty good judge of character but this time he had really slipped up.

I didn't know how long Rachel had been standing there or how much she'd heard. Right then, I didn't give a hoot. And the worst thing was—she was wearing the silk dressing-gown we bought Mum for her birthday. I got a fleeting vision of it, flowing down and over Rachel's feet, done up to the neck, the collar turned up, a riot of white hair round her head. She buried her face in Ro's thick fur and murmured something else.

I gave her the worst black look I could muster, launched myself up the stairs, along the landing, and into my room. I slammed the door so hard it was a wonder the house didn't crack in half. All the way up I could feel her eyes following me. It was as if she could see right into my brain. Well, if she can, I thought angrily, I hope she'll know what I'm thinking. I hope she'll realize I know exactly what she is even if Mum doesn't.

In my room, I keyed in Jake's web-site address. He'd gone out. That really was the last straw. My best friend deserting me in my hour of need! Wasn't there any justice in the World?

2

Later the doorphone buzzed twice.

First, Damien's friend's mother bringing him back from a day at the play-dome. I heard Mum telling him to thank her for taking him. I could just imagine him shuffling his feet on the mat and mumbling something. I heard him run up the stairs and chuck his sports bag on his bed then run down again.

I wondered what he'd think of Rachel. He'd probably get her with his zapper before she even had a chance to say hello. Damien is never seen without his zapper, stunning everyone as a matter of course. Friend or foe.

Then the buzzer went again. I heard Jake's voice echoing through the speaker.

'I'll let him in!' I dashed down the stairs, wrenched open the door and pulled him inside.

'You'll never guess what?' I blurted out half-way up stairs to my room.

'A Misfit!' He laughed when I told him. 'Cool! Has your mum given up cats then?'

I chucked an empty cola can at him. 'It's not cool. It's disgusting . . . and dangerous. You wait till you see her.'

Jake lounged on my bed. His dark hair stuck up in spikes where he'd taken off his baseball cap and chucked it on the dressing-table. I often wish Jake had some kind of dress sense. He was wearing a bright pink all-weather survival jacket with a pair of grey sportsuit trousers that had got plastered with mud from his bike. Mostly I tried to ignore his complete lack of style. After all, he does have a brilliant brain, good taste in rock music, and a

16

fantastic sense of humour even if he does laugh at me when he should be taking me seriously.

He sat up. 'OK, tell me about her.'

'I don't know anything about her, nor does Mum. All I *do* know is that she stinks!'

I sighed and lay back with my hands behind my head. I stared at the crimson and blue symbols I'd painted on the ceiling. Mum had exploded when she first saw them even though she'd said I could do what I liked with my room. She said she had never seen anything like them. Neither had I. That's why I'd painted them. I don't know where they came from. They just came into my head from nowhere.

Jake chuckled again. Then he looked more serious.

'Your mum's taking a hell of a risk.'

'Tell me about it!' I said. 'Anyway, she says Misfits rarely get out of the City limits.'

He looked thoughtful. 'She could be a Drifter. I saw the police rounding up a bunch of them on the news last week. They'd made a tree-camp somewhere and the police were tearing it down and loading the people into the backs of vans . . . kids and dogs . . . everything.'

A Drifter! Why hadn't I thought of that? Probably because Drifters usually go around in groups and Rachel was all by herself.

'I bet that's what she is, then! She's got separated from the rest of her band.'

I sat up. I suddenly wanted to change the subject. I didn't want to think about where people went when their homes had been torn down. As long as they didn't invade us I didn't really care. I'm a great one for putting my head in the sand.

'Anyway,' I said. 'What are you doing here?'

'I got bored.'

I grinned. 'So you thought you'd come to dinner?'

Jake's mum is a nurse working twenty-hour shifts in the City emergency hospital so he was alone most of the time.

'Yep,' he said.

I pulled a face. 'I hope you don't regret it.'

'What? Because of Rachel? To be honest I'm curious about her.' Jake is even nosier than me.

'So am I,' I admitted. 'But that doesn't mean I want her in my house.'

'Anyway,' he went on. 'I shouldn't worry. It's probably just one of your mum's schemes. She'll feed her then send her on her way.'

'Like she feeds the cats, you mean?' I fiddled with the corner of the duvet. 'Like they stay for ever!'

'She might not be as bad as you think.'

'You wait,' I said although I didn't really know why. It's really stupid to hate someone when you don't even know them. Somehow I just couldn't help it.

I did feel better, though. Jake always had that effect on me. He's a great one for putting things into perspective. He sees things rationally while I fly off the handle. Maybe he was right. She *was* just one of Mum's schemes. Maybe she would freshen up, eat up, then drift off somewhere else.

We were generally messing around when the door shot open. Damien stood there, legs apart like an alien ready to exterminate life as we knew it.

He screwed up his freckly snub-nose. 'Mum says dinner's ready and is Jake staying?'

'Yes, he is,' I told him. 'Now buzz off.'

'Buzz off yourself.' Damien zapped me then disappeared, racing down the stairs, shooting everything in sight. Jake chased after him, zapping him back. I sighed. Jake's crazy about sci-fi but I would have thought he'd have grown out of the zapping stage by now.

My dad must have been starving too because he surfaced just as we reached the bottom of the stairs. He sniffed the air.

'I smell one of Mum's gourmet meals.' He made a feeble attempt at a joke—my mum is the worst cook in the universe. As he closed his door I caught sight of his four screens blinking away. He's been stuck into a project for months now and has hardly been out of his room.

He said 'Hi' to Jake.

'Have you met your visitor yet?' Jake asked.

Dad frowned and shook his head. 'No, what visitor?'

Jake told him in spite of me kicking his ankle and hissing at him to shut up. I knew explanations would sound better coming from Mum.

Dad shook his head incredulously and scratched his beard. 'Your mother's gone mad,' he said.

He pushed open the kitchen door. They were all waiting. Mum. Damien. Rachel. The cats were spread around Rachel's feet like furry slippers. The TV was blaring out a game show but no one was watching it.

Archie was laying the table, shuffling to and fro with knives and forks. Rachel looked at us apprehensively as we walked in. First at me, then Jake, then Dad. Flicking her eyes up then dropping her gaze quickly as if the sight of our faces burned her pupils. She was wearing a green sweatshirt of mum's and a pair of old jeans. My old jeans! Ones I'd chucked into the recycling bin. Her fingers were fiddling with her spoon. White hands, elegant fingers, pink nails now the grime had been scrubbed away. She had scraped her riot of hair back. Grey wisps had escaped and drifted round her high cheekbones. One wandered across her small, pointed nose and she brushed it away absent-mindedly.

I drew in my breath. For an old person she was quite beautiful. I felt a shock wave surf across my skin, icy fingertips freezing my flesh as they went. She looked at me and knew how I was feeling. She still had that aura about her, clearer now I could see her face properly. Pale gold and shining and seemed to hover all around her.

Dad was staring at her, his mouth open. Then he grabbed the remote and switched off the Set. A sure sign trouble was brewing.

19

I dropped my eyes then plonked myself down in my usual place. I pulled a stool out for Jake and waited for Dad to explode.

'Hi, everyone,' Jake said in a strangled voice.

'Jake,' Mum said as if we didn't already know his name. 'Good to see you.' She was talking to him but glancing at Dad. Dad was still staring at Rachel. His dark, bushy eyebrows had knitted together in a tight, black knot of anger.

'You too,' Jake was saying feebly.

'George.' Mum was still looking at Dad. Damien was switching his gaze from one to the other as if he was watching a tennis match on the sports channel.

'Jake . . . ' Mum went on. 'This is Rachel.'

I do like Jake, I saw Mum key in once when she was e-mailing one of her Net friends. He might look like a scarecrow but he's got really good manners. So refreshing in this day and age. Most young people have such an attitude problem.

I knew she meant me.

I spied from under my lashes. Rachel touched Jake's extended fingers across the table, smiled softly but didn't speak.

'George?' Mum was still looking at Dad apprehensively.

But he couldn't be bothered with niceties. 'I've never met a Misfit before,' he said candidly.

'George!' Mum protested as if *misfit* was a dirty word. Which, as far as most people were concerned, it was. 'Rachel is my guest . . . '

But Rachel met his eye. 'Misfit?'

She looked like a normal person now. She wasn't old at all. Not *really* old. Eighty perhaps, maybe a bit more? Her skin was shiny, wrinkled, pale as paper, like a City dweller who hardly ever gets the chance to go out in the sun.

'Wow!' Damien leant forward and captured a bit of bread. His sleeve dangled in his dinner. He sucked off

20

the gravy, then licked round his mouth. 'Is that what you are? I've been doing Misfits in my social history.'

But Rachel still looked puzzled.

'A person who doesn't fit into the social environment,' Jake explained. 'A nonconformist, a freak, a mutation.'

Damien burst out laughing, spitting bits of gravy-soaked bread all over the place.

Dad didn't say anything else. He just breathed deeply, squeezed his lips together in that tight white line that heralded a big row between him and Mum. The signs were obvious.

Rachel was looking shocked at what Jake had said. I suddenly, oddly, felt sorry for her.

'OK, you lot,' Mum said loudly. 'Shut up and eat.'

'But is she one?' Damien nagged.

We all stared at her.

'No.' She took a deep breath. 'That's not what I am. At least . . . I don't think so.'

Dad snorted and threw Mum a vampire glance. Pretending to have lost her memory? That made things even worse.

Suddenly, I couldn't bear it. I couldn't bear sitting at the table with this old woman, Mum and Dad throwing daggers at each other with their eyes because of her. I hate rows.

I stood up.

'Where are you going?' Mum looked startled.

'I'm not hungry,' I said.

'Yes, you are.' She obviously knew the state of my stomach better than I did. 'Stay and eat.'

I sat down, red in the face. Jake threw me a glance of sympathy. Rachel had lowered her eyes and was gobbling her dinner as if there was no tomorrow.

She finished miles before anyone else.

'That was lovely, thank you.'

Damien almost choked. No one has ever called Mum's cooking *lovely* before.

Rachel wiped her face on her napkin as Archie

hovered to take away her plate. Then I swear I saw her wink one eye at Damien.

I was still trying to figure out whether she had or not when she got up. 'Will you excuse me?' she asked. 'I'm really tired.'

Damien was still giggling until Jake kicked him under the table. Then he frowned and stuck out his bottom lip and rubbed his ankle. 'You wait!' he hissed.

'Of course. Sleep well,' Mum was still smiling like an idiot. 'Tomorrow is an out-work day for me but Kari and George will be here.' She had to go into her headquarters sometimes for face-to-face meetings with the corporation she worked for.

'I'll be here too,' Damien piped up.

'No, you won't, you're coming with me.'

Damien stuck out his bottom lip. 'I hate that crèche place, it's for kids.'

'Well, that's what you are,' I said. I leant across Jake and ruffled Damien's hair.

He shied away, scowling. 'Get off, do-lally Kari.'

'We're going to Bluelake,' I added quickly, ignoring Damien. The last thing I wanted was to hang around the house with *her* here. 'Aren't we, Jake?'

'Er . . . yeah,' he said.

'I can't take you,' Mum said. 'I've almost used up my month's fuel ration as it is.'

'It's OK,' I said, 'we'll get the Link. Won't we, Jake?'

'Yeah,' Jake said.

'You be careful,' Dad warned.

'We will,' Jake said.

My stomach turned over with excitement. It was months since I'd been anywhere. The shops, the lights, the people, the games arcades . . . they were brilliant. I loved living at the Cottage but it was great to get out once in a while.

'Thank you for the meal.' Rachel had been listening to all this. Now she put her chair back up to the table and slipped out of the room. The cats went too. Following her silently like a little band of pilgrims, tails waving in the air like banners.

A babble broke out when she had gone. Damien went to switch on the TV. Archie whirred into action again and started clearing the table even though Dad hadn't finished.

'Look!' Mum shouted above the noise. 'I've said she can stay as long as she likes.' She glanced sideways at Dad. He had a face like one of the thunderheads that gather over the top of the hills just before a storm.

I groaned. 'But what happens if she stays for *ever*.'

Mum shrugged. 'So be it.'

'She can be our granny,' Damien piped up.

I looked at him in horror as everyone, surprisingly even Dad, burst out laughing.

3

When we'd watched the end of the game-show Jake said he'd got to go.

I went outside with him. The rain had cleared. Everything seemed sparkling and new, even in the light of the fading day. The ghost of a twilight moon hung in the inky cloudless sky.

'There you are,' Jake said. 'It's not going to rain for ever.'

I laughed and punched his arm. 'What did you think of her?' I asked.

'Rachel?' He frowned. 'She's weird.'

'You're not kidding,' I said. 'Did you notice her eyes?'

'Yes.' He gazed at me then grinned. 'She's another one who would have been burnt as a witch five hundred years ago.'

I didn't know why but I shuddered when he said that.

We said goodbye at the gate. I keyed in the night code and he went through.

'See you tomorrow.' He got on his bike and pedalled off.

'Take care,' I called.

I watched him disappear down the road. In the distance, the City lights made the sky glow orange. The trees were silhouetted against it, black outlines against a backdrop of fire. Green, red, and blue eyes winked across the horizon as planes left the airport to fly to all corners of the World.

I stood a minute, looking at the dark shadowed hills. They looked even more mysterious. Like the humped backs of great extinct whales basking on the horizon. I took deep breaths of air. It was evening-fresh, the worst of the pollution blown away for a while by the rain and wind.

For some reason Rachel crashed into my thoughts. I suddenly tried to imagine what it must be like. Not fitting in, not *belonging*, being *different*. No home, no safe-house, no shelter from the rain or wind or snow. Sleeping stone cold on pavements, under bridges, in derelict buildings, in cardboard boxes . . . anywhere you could.

I pushed the images from my mind, went back inside, closed the door and keyed in the code.

In the kitchen, the air was blue.

'You're mad, Asia!' Dad was dodging around as Archie stacked the dishwasher. 'You're putting us all at risk.'

'I know. I'm sorry but it was just something I had to do. I can't explain it.'

'Where the hell did she come from? She's probably escaped from a loony bin somewhere.'

'I don't know,' Mum shouted.

'Well, didn't you ask her?'

'No, I didn't like to. She seemed dazed, disorientated . . . all she told me was her name.'

Dad snorted with derision. 'She could be a danger to us, to the children.'

'Yes, I know.' It wasn't like Mum to be agreeing with him.

'And what's that thing she's got round her wrist? It could be a medi-alert . . . she could have some contagious condition. These people have no access to immunization programmes, you know.'

'I know, I'm not stupid.'

Archie had closed the washer door. It began to hum and swish, merrily oblivious to the tornado raging round the room.

The kitchen door opened suddenly. I dodged back. They would hate it if they knew I was eavesdropping.

'You'd better get rid of her, Asia.' Dad came out. Shouting. He headed back into his office. 'Now! And if you won't tell her to go, I damn well will! And you'd better lock up the wine,' he yelled over his shoulder as he went through the door. 'And the tranquillizers. They'll disappear faster than a packet of chocolate buttons.'

'I won't do any such thing!' Mum stood with her hands on her hips. She swore, made a finger-sign at Dad's departing figure, stormed along to *her* office, and slammed the door. Hard.

It was then that I saw Rachel standing at the top of the stairs. She was cuddling Bones in her arms. He was asleep. It looked almost as if he was smiling. His soft white face was covered in contentment. I went up and stood in front of her.

'Oh, dear.' She looked upset. 'I've really put the cat among the pigeons.'

'They're always rowing anyway,' I told her.

'Do you think I should go?'

I really didn't know why she was asking me.

I shrugged. 'It's up to you,' I said although of course it wasn't up to her at all. What I *should* have said was 'Yes. Buzz off . . . now.'

She walked to the window and stared out at the sky. There was a blizzard of stars now. They stretched luminously right across the heavens to the rim of the galaxy. She had a strange expression on her face as she turned back to me. I noticed for the first time that she *was* wearing a bracelet of some kind. My dad must have seen it when we were having dinner. It looked like some kind of electronic tagging device. Or maybe Dad was right? Perhaps it was a medi-tag to warn you the wearer was HIV positive or was some kind of plague carrier or something.

I took a step back, away from her. If she noticed, she didn't say a word.

Bones opened one sleepy eye, yawned in her arms, then went straight back to sleep.

Rachel saw me staring at her bracelet and tucked it quickly out of sight.

'You like living here, don't you, Kari?' she said out of the blue.

'Yes,' I said. Then I found myself telling her how we came to be here. I really didn't know why. Half an hour ago I couldn't even bear to speak to her. There was something about her gentle way of asking you things that made you open up.

'Mum and Dad wanted us to grow up away from the City,' I said. 'We came here when I was three.'

'Yes,' she said, gazing at me with her strange eyes.

'Thirteen years ago,' I rattled on. I didn't know why I was telling her the history of my life. 'Two years before Damien was born. They were lucky to get this place. It had managed to survive the craze for knocking down old buildings.'

'Oh,' Rachel said.

'It had been empty for years. Since the station closed and the line was abandoned.' I remembered how we had to live in a trailer in the garden while Mum and Dad repaired the Cottage and made it habitable.

'How long ago was that?' she asked.

I shrugged. 'I don't know . . . years before the millennium.'

I glanced at my watch. It was time for my favourite teen-soap and I'd have hated to miss the beginning.

'You lived in the . . . City . . . before?' she asked.

'In the suburbs,' I said. 'Although I don't remember it.'

'It must have seemed strange for your parents at first,' she said.

'Yes.'

I remembered seeing Mum tell someone that something had happened when they first moved out here that almost made her give up and return to their suburban skyblock. Something that had obviously been traumatic for her.

'It was a terrible time,' she had put. 'And it made me realize the countryside held just as many dangers as the City.'

She didn't explain what had made her think that. She just went on to tell her Net-friend how Dad had persuaded her to stay and how she loved it out here now, how safe she felt, and how she wouldn't want to live anywhere else.

Rachel's eyes were washing over the walls, the ancient oak beams. She ran her fingertips along the windowsill, then up over the shutters, feeling the texture of their wooden surface as if it was something completely new to her. 'I wonder when this was built?' she said.

'Nineteen hundred,' I said, knowing exactly. 'A hundred and fifty years ago.'

'Goodness,' she said. She looked at me. 'Do you think your dad can be persuaded to let me stay?'

'I doubt it,' I said. 'He never changes his mind.'

'Perhaps I could sleep outside?'

I shook my head. 'I don't think that's a very good idea.'

Rachel sighed. 'Oh, dear,' she said.

'Where will you go?' I suddenly saw a picture of her, tramping off with her old bags into the sunset. To the City maybe where she could get mugged, raped, killed for the clothes on her back and end up dying in some garbage-filled gutter.

But she had a far-away look in her eyes and didn't answer. She just turned and swept back to her room. I stared after her and suddenly, stupidly felt like crying.

Something else too . . . all my preconceived ideas suddenly seemed to fly out of the window and I knew with a sudden, crazy certainty that Rachel was none of the things I had first thought her to be.

I was still standing there when Damien tore out of his bedroom. He shoved past me and went to bang on her door. She called 'Come in' and he disappeared inside. I could hear them talking. Her voice soft and murmuring.

28

His, high and excited. For some silly reason I felt a stab of jealousy. There was something about Rachel . . . her voice . . . the gentle aura that surrounded her. Whatever it was I couldn't stop thinking about her. I'd felt like that when I first met Jake but that was different. He's a really interesting, friendly, cool guy; Rachel's a peculiar, eccentric, mysterious, smelly old woman.

I went into my room and closed the door. I went to the drawer, took out my flute, then sat cross-legged on the bed. I touched the rare, smooth box-wood of my flute. I felt its coolness under my fingers. I put it to my lips and played a soft, white tune. One I'd made up years ago when I was a little kid. 'Winter,' I'd called it because it was the year we had loads of snow.

I messed around with a few other melodies for a while, then, feeling better, I put my flute away and sat down in front of my screen. I keyed in Jake's address. Then I heard Rachel's door open and footsteps along the corridor. I put the machine on hold and went to peep out of my door. Rachel and Damien were skulking off into his room. I thought he was probably wanting to show her his zapper. I didn't know why but I felt quite yellow with envy. There were lots of things I'd like to have shown her. My flute, my collection of old books, the fossil-shells our astronaut uncle brought me back from one of his trips into space.

Jake was still busy. He was probably talking to one of his Net-friends about the internal workings of old combustion engines, or space rockets, or quantum physics, or something else he knows loads about. He stays up half the night doing it sometimes.

I accessed the teen-soap, watched it for ten minutes, got bored with the same old storylines then tried again.

This time I got him. I told him about Mum and Dad's rumpus.

'Your dad's right,' he said. He was munching a peanut butter sandwich and wearing the green '*Save Our Planet*' cap I'd bought him.

I sighed. 'Trust you men to stick together.'

'It's not that.' Jake tipped his cap to the back of his head. 'But he *is* right and you know it.'

'It just seems rotten,' I said. 'It wouldn't hurt if she stayed a few days.'

Jake chuckled. 'You've changed your tune.'

'I know.'

'Why?' he asked. 'An hour or so ago she was smelly and horrible and you wanted her out.'

I shrugged. 'I don't know. There's just something about her. I don't think she *is* a con-woman or even a Misfit or a Drifter.'

'What was she doing on the road, then?'

I shook my head. 'Search me.'

Jake looked thoughtful. 'Maybe you *could* pass her off as your gran?'

I laughed. 'No one's likely to believe that, are they? Do *you* know anyone who's got a grandparent living with them?'

'Nope,' he said with his mouth full.

When I'd logged off I went to eavesdrop at Damien's door. They were still in there. I was pink with curiosity. I *had* to see what they were up to.

When I went in, Rachel was sitting in front of his machine. He was showing her how to use it. He turned, scowling, when he heard me. She turned too, smiled a secret kind of smile at me, then turned back to the screen.

'Buzz off,' Damien said but I ignored him.

He was showing Rachel how to log on, how to access the web and browse around to see what's happening. How to bring up the mail reader. She sat next to him, watching, then leaned forward. Her fingers flew over the keyboard as she accessed the web and began to browse around.

I suddenly went cold. She was using Damien's computer as if she had been doing it all her life.

'Thank you, Damien.' She logged off suddenly. 'I

30

think that's enough. Kari,' she said. 'Can you spare five minutes? I'd like to talk to you.'

I shrugged. 'Sure.'

Before I followed her out, Damien said, 'She says she's used one before.' He must have known I was puzzled.

'Oh?' I said. Inside I was feeling strange and curious. Misfits *never* got access to computers. They weren't allowed in techno-centres, or libraries, or anywhere like that. And Drifters despised technology. It was part of their philosophy to live without it. So . . . ? Where had Rachel used one before? I began to think she was completely surrounded in a fog of mystery. Just like those figures in my dream. And it all went to prove she was definitely not what she seemed.

Damien had turned back to his screen and accessed one of his interactives. He forgot all about me in his determination to zap as many Maze monsters as possible in the time allowed.

Rachel wasn't in her room when I looked. Then, when I'd gone into my own room to close the shutters I spotted her out in the garden. She was sitting on one of the seats, leaning forward, her elbows on her knees. She was staring up at the sky. She had her tatty old coat slung around her shoulders. A breeze eddied round her, wisps of hair softly settling on the pearly skin of her cheeks.

I pulled a sweater from my drawer, dragged it on, slipped down the stairs and out of the door. As I went past Dad's office I heard him talking to someone on his videophone. He was still working even though it was really late.

'Rachel?'

My voice made her jump. She turned swiftly, something like fear hovering round her. When she saw it was me, she relaxed and patted the place beside her.

'Ah, Kari,' she said. 'Come and sit with me.'

I sat, leaning back with my legs outstretched. I

glanced sideways. She wasn't looking at me now, just staring up at the sky.

'I heard you playing your flute,' she said.

'Yeah?' I didn't know what else to say.

'It was beautiful.'

'Thanks.' Playing the flute was so much part of me that sometimes I forgot other people could hear it too.

'You have a great gift,' she said.

I shrugged. 'That's what people tell me.' It was because no one had ever taught me to play. I have just always been able to do it. My uncle bought me a recorder when I was really small and when they found I could play it they bought me a flute. I've played ever since.

Rachel and I sat in silence for a while. Then I asked her something that had been bugging me ever since she arrived.

'Where were you going when Mum found you?' I asked. 'This road doesn't go anywhere. Are you a Drifter got separated from your band?' I glanced sideways at her.

The question seemed to take her by surprise. I had sat down close to her. I could smell Mum's herbal shampoo she'd used to wash her hair. She didn't answer at first. Instead she picked up my hand and rubbed it between her own, absent-mindedly as if she was trying to warm it when it wasn't even cold. Her fingers were smooth and soft. Her sleeve fell back and I saw her bracelet properly for the first time. It was made of a bright metal I'd never seen before. I reached out a finger and touched it. It was warm from the heat of her arm and seemed to reflect a dozen shades of white moonlight. There was something engraved on it. She dropped my hand and tucked the bracelet out of sight before I could make out what it was.

I asked her again about being a Drifter because she hadn't answered and seemed to have forgotten I'd even asked her a question.

'A Drifter?' she said in that strange way she had of repeating what you had said as if she had never heard the word before. 'No, I'm not a Drifter.'

'Don't tell me you're a tourist,' I giggled. 'If you are you chose a rotten day to come.'

She shook her head. 'A tourist? No-oo, I don't think so,' she said.

'Something's happened to you to make you lose your memory.' I sat forward, tucking my hands under my bottom, my shoulders hunched. That's definitely what had happened to her. 'You've been attacked, hit on the head or something, and you've got amnesia,' I said. 'You know what you're *not*, but not what you *are*, if you see what I mean. It's pretty obvious, isn't it?'

'That I've been bonked on the head,' she smiled softly. 'Can you see any cuts and bruises?'

'No.' I had to admit I couldn't.

She unconsciously tucked a strand of her hair behind her ear. Then she looked at her other hand. Her smile faded and a frown took its place. It was almost as if she couldn't believe her hand belonged to her . . . as if she had only just noticed she'd got it. She spread her fingers out; there was a ring on one, a fat gold band. She began fiddling with it, turning it round and round as if she was trying to screw her finger off. I wondered how someone like her got hold of a gold ring. It was only afterwards I realized she hadn't answered me when I'd asked her about where she had been going when Mum picked her up.

She took hold of my hand again. 'Kari,' she said. 'I did really want to talk to you about something.' She broke off, then did something really strange. She pointed up to the stars.

'Look,' she said. 'Starlight City.'

The night was so clear you could imagine you could almost see the curve of the World.

I giggled. Maybe she was nutty after all?

'Starlight City? What's that?'

33

'Don't you think that's what the night sky looks like?' She pointed again. 'Look, the Plough, the Great Bear, Cassiopeia, Andromeda—all regions of a great metropolis.'

I stared upwards and it was as if I was really seeing the stars for the first time in my life. I knew they'd all got names but couldn't tell you which ones were which. I imagined a great galaxy of cities with lights shining from towers and steeples, skyblocks, domes and airports. I blinked and the vision dissolved.

'Don't you agree?' Rachel was saying softly in my ear.

'Yes.' I shivered suddenly. 'I've never thought of it like that before.'

'It's good to see things with new eyes,' she said. 'Sometimes it just needs someone to point the way.'

I went on looking at the stars. I felt really weird. Rachel had made me see something I'd never seen before. How she'd done it I didn't know. All I did know was that it was really spooky. It wasn't the same kind of creepy feeling I'd had when she first arrived. It was more like my dream-feeling. The feeling that my life was about to be changed for ever.

I suddenly found myself saying, 'Stay tonight, Rachel. It won't hurt.'

'What about your dad?'

'He won't know. He hardly ever comes out of his room except to eat.'

'All right, but it looks as if I'll have to go tomorrow.'

'Where?' I asked. 'Where will you go?'

'The City,' she said.

'The City! Have you got any idea what it's like there?' I said, suddenly scared. 'You won't last five minutes.'

She gazed at me with a real burning intensity in her eyes. 'It'll be all right. I've got friends . . . But first I need to—'

It was then we heard Mum calling and whatever it was Rachel was going to say died on her lips.

'Come on.' She got up. 'I'll talk to you later.'

I followed her through the door feeling annoyed. I could have quite happily stayed out in the garden all night.

Mum came along the hall to meet us. 'Kari! I thought you were in bed.'

'We've been having a chat,' Rachel explained before I could say a word.

'That's nice.' Mum fiddled with her ear-ring as she always does when she's stressed. 'Rachel, I need to have a talk to you.' She gave me a look that meant disappear . . . fast.

She took Rachel's arm and led her into the front room. I heard the TV go off then the murmur of voices. I put my ear to the door but they were speaking so softly I couldn't make out what they were saying.

'Goodnight, Kari,' Archie said from his corner in the hall as I went upstairs to my room.

In bed, I couldn't sleep. I'd accessed a relaxer-file but even the soft flute-music and the voice spouting gentle poetry didn't help.

I turned over, trying to get comfortable. For some reason I felt really miserable.

Finally I put the machine in standby and lay there listening to the far distant hum of the cars queuing to get through the City turnpikes. The chug-chug of their engines carried all the way here at night.

I suddenly imagined Rachel, trying to get past the armed patrols, getting lost in the maze of streets. I thought she probably wouldn't last five minutes. She seemed fragile and vulnerable with none of the toughness that vagabonds need to survive. And it would be our fault for making her leave.

She would be gone and we would never have had the chance to know anything about her.

In the distance I heard the whine of police sirens, the drumming of a helicopter on night-patrol. On clear evenings you could always hear them easily but tonight they seemed closer than ever.

Then I heard something else. The sad strains of a sonata echoing up from the hall. Mum must have finished her chat with Rachel and was playing the piano. I listened for a while, the sad melody weaving itself around me like a lullaby.

I turned over again and drifted into a restless, mixed-up, dream-filled sleep.

4

I woke up with a jump that almost tipped me out of bed.
Gone midnight. What in the World had woken me? I'd
been dreaming again. Those eerie figures I'd dreamed
about before. They were coming out of the darkness
towards me but this time I was walking towards them—
unafraid.

As soon as I opened my eyes I realized I hadn't got
round to closing my shutters. A stream of moonlight
trickled across my bed and down on to the floor.

I strained my ears, trying to make out what had
disturbed me. There was no sound but the ceaseless and
distant hum of the City.

Then, suddenly, my videophone gave an impatient
bleep. I scrambled out of bed. Jake. Looking serious for
a change, his face pale, his hair all over the place. He
was still wearing his day clothes.

'What's up?' I'd never seen him look so worried before.

When he told me, my heart turned over. I felt white
with cold, as if someone had sliced the top of my head
off with a scalpel made of ice. Police investigators had
been to his house. Three of them, more in vehicles
waiting outside, and the heli-patrol hovering overhead.

'They asked if we'd seen a woman, dressed like a
vagrant.'

I breathed in. 'Rachel?'

'Had to be.' Jake looked more grim than I'd ever seen
him. 'They questioned us for ages. Luckily I hadn't said
anything to Mum about her and she didn't know what
I'd been doing all day.'

'What did you say?' I asked. My heart was thudding. I'd seen stories on the News-net about police interrogation procedures.

'I just played innocent,' Jake said. 'Told them I didn't know a thing.'

'Did they believe you?'

He shrugged again. 'Looks like it. They seemed satisfied anyway.' He leaned forward. 'Look, Kari, they're working their way to your place. If Rachel's still there you'd better warn her . . . get her out if you can.'

'Yes, she is still here.' My brain whirled. How long would they take to get here? Jake's house . . . two more houses, two factory-farms . . . then us. A couple of hours . . . half an hour . . . there was no telling.

But there was something I didn't understand.

'What do they want her for?'

'No idea,' Jake said. 'But they were deadly serious and you're wasting time, Kari.'

Damien came out of his room as I sped along the landing. My brain was still spinning. Where could Rachel hide where they couldn't find her?

'What you up to?' Damien rubbed sleep from his eyes. His red hair stuck up as if he'd been electrocuted.

'Nothing,' I hissed, scared Mum and Dad would hear.

'Yes, you are.'

I knew he'd keep on so I told him what Jake had said.

He frowned. 'What do they want a raggy old Misfit for?'

'No idea,' I hissed. 'Now get back to bed.'

Damien refused to budge. His zapper appeared miraculously from the sleeve of his sleepsuit.

'What's she done?' he said.

'I don't know,' I hissed, 'and I don't really care right now. Damien, they musn't find her here,' I added urgently. 'They'll cart her off to the loony bin.'

Suddenly, her door opened. She was wearing an old sleepsuit that Mum had given her. Her hair was a wild fuzz round her head. Her eyes were wide with concern. A tangle of snoozing cats cluttered her duvet.

'What's going on?'

I bundled her back inside, dragging Damien along with us. I closed the door softly then began explaining.

'You've got to go, Rachel,' Damien said. He had opened the shutters and was looking out of the window, peering up the road to see if anyone was coming. 'They'll sling you in the loony bin.'

'Shut up, Damien,' I hissed.

But Rachel was already stuffing some things frantically into one of her carrier bags. Some books, a box, three pairs of socks. A strange black wedge-shaped object she brought out from under her pillow.

She dragged on the old sweatshirt and my jeans over her sleepsuit. Then she pulled on the ratty old boots she had on when she first arrived. She reached up into the cupboard and took down her coat and scarf.

I helped. My stomach was churning with fear. I could feel her terror too. In fact I could *see* it. A deep red shimmer round her whole body, sparking now and then as she moved swiftly to and fro.

Damien perched on the bed among the cats. They had woken up and were pacing up and down the duvet anxiously, their tails high in the air. Rachel turned to say something but Damien got in first.

'Why do they want you?' he asked, chewing the end of his zapper.

She didn't answer but said instead, 'I shouldn't have accepted your mum's offer, it's put you all in danger. I'm sorry.'

'It doesn't matter,' I blurted out before I could stop myself. My brain must be doing a blip. It *did* matter that the police were on their way to question us and maybe turn the place over.

Rachel was wringing her hands together, looking round anxiously. 'I need to hide,' she said as if a secret passage might suddenly open up in one of the walls.

39

'Hide?' Damien said. 'You don't want to hide, you want to run.'

She ignored him again and clutched my arm. 'Can you think of anywhere, Kari?'

I shook my head. 'There's nowhere that they wouldn't find you. They'll bring in trackerbeams, heatseekers . . . ' My stomach was twisted with the thought.

'The old station,' she said suddenly. 'Would they look there?'

'Might do,' Damien said. He was sounding mighty calm for someone about to get a visit from the police. He put the zapper down and sat on his hands, swinging his legs to and fro. 'A crimmo hid there once and they got him. I saw them kill him with their zappers.'

'Guns,' I said. 'Zappers are only toys.'

'Guns, then,' Damien said. 'Anyway he was stone dead.'

It was true. The man had been a terrorist on the run. It had been ages ago, when Damien was only a toddler. I was surprised he'd remembered. I can't remember anything that happened to me before I was about six.

Rachel was pacing up and down. 'Where, then?' she was saying.

Suddenly she turned to us. Her face lit up. 'The tunnel,' she said.

A ghost of a thought flitted past my mind. The tunnel . . . how did she know about *that*? Then I forgot how puzzled I was and answered her question. 'It's all bricked up.' I shook my head. 'There's no way in.'

'I'll find one.' Rachel picked up her bag.

'Damien,' I said. 'Get back to bed, I'll go with Rachel.'

'Not likely,' he said. 'You're not going without me.'

He was as pig-headed as Dad and I knew nothing would make him change his mind. And in the time we spent arguing about it, Rachel could be on her way.

'It's all right,' she said. 'I can find it on my own.'

But I couldn't let her go out there in the dark alone. 'No,' I said. 'We'll come with you.'

She shook her head. 'It's too dangerous, please, Kari.'

But I was stubborn too. I couldn't let her try to find the tunnel in the dark. She could wander around for ages and never locate it. Damien and I knew *exactly* where it was.

I grabbed Damien's arm. 'Go and get dressed then and if you wake Mum and Dad I'll kill you.'

I ran on tiptoe to my room. I chucked on my sweater and jeans and all-weather jacket, dragged on my boots and was back in a trice. Damien was already there, his sportsuit thrown on over his sleepsuit, zapper rammed in his belt, his Euro-United football cap stuck on his head.

We didn't dare activate the lights so we crept down the stairs in the dark. Moonshine pierced the stained-glass window making a shaft of colours on the wall.

At the bottom I trod on Ro. His yowl echoed up the stairs and along the landing. We crouched, holding our breath. I put my arms over my head and squeezed my eyes shut. I waited but nothing happened.

When I did dare look up, I heard an upstairs door open. My heart sank. Mum. She would go mad if she saw what we were up to.

'It's OK, it's Rachel,' Damien whispered. 'She went back up. She forgot something.'

I swore under my breath. Didn't she know that every minute counted if she was to get away? We'd lost enough time already.

Then she appeared at the top. She reached us, apologizing. 'Sorry,' she whispered. 'I'm ready now.'

I grabbed her hand. I felt her fingers tighten in mine.

'Let me help.' I reached for her bag. It looked really heavy. Maybe she did have the crown jewels inside after all.

'No, it's all right,' she said hastily. 'I can manage.'

We dodged past Dad's door. Inside, his snores rumbled round the room. It was nothing unusual for

41

him to fall asleep at his screens. Mum usually went to rouse him so he could go up to bed but tonight she had left him there. She was probably punishing him for the row they'd had. He would wake up stiff as a board in the morning and in a foul temper.

I crept into the kitchen and grabbed a torch from the drawer. Back in the hall, I de-activated the night-code and immobilized the alarms and lights. The door opened with a heart-stopping clunk. The night and the darkness flowed in.

We waited, in case anyone had woken. We held our breath for so long that I swear we were all blue in the face by the time we let it out.

'Come on.' I pulled Rachel through.

Damien hung back. 'I'm scared,' he wailed. 'I don't like the dark.'

Rachel took his hand. 'Come on,' she said softly. 'The darkness can be your friend if you let it.'

We closed the door quietly behind us and crept down the path.

I saw Rachel glance up at the sky. Clouds skimmed the moon and stars. A wind had sprung up. It touched the branches of the trees and jerked them stiffly around. Long shadows danced across the garden as I keyed in the code and the front gate swung open. I glanced over my shoulder, looking back at the house.

Total darkness. I breathed a sigh of relief. We hadn't disturbed anyone except the poor old cat.

We were just about to dive across the road when Rachel gave a quick intake of breath.

'There's someone coming!'

'It's them!' Damien began to cry.

'Shut *up*.' I clicked off the torch, scared stiff.

A light was coming down the road towards us. Not fast but approaching steadily, winking and twinkling in the dark like a rapidly moving star.

I pulled Damien's sleeve. My heart was thudding in my chest. 'Come on . . . run!'

Then a lone voice hissed towards us.

'Hey, you lot. Wait for me.'

Jake. I breathed a sigh of relief and heard Rachel do the same.

'Jake!' Damien cried as if Jake was the saviour he had been waiting for. 'We're going to the old tunnel.'

'Shut *up*, Damien,' I hissed. 'Do you want the whole World to know?'

Rachel had gone on ahead. Across the ditch and over the fence, hurrying, running, tripping, scrambling up the embankment. Her old coat flapped around her like the wings of a night bird. She seemed to be able to see in the dark.

Jake slung his bike into the hedge and we all scrambled after her.

'How is she going to get inside?' Jake panted when we'd caught her up.

'No idea,' I gasped.

Rachel stood at the top, her hair streaming in the wind. I looked up. My breath caught in my throat. She looked really strange, silhouetted against the stars. Like some brave, invincible warrior-queen from the past when only a few hours ago she had been a hopeless, homeless Misfit invading our home. I could hardly believe the change in her.

'Hurry!' she called. The wind took her voice and carried it to all four corners of the World.

In the distance I could hear the ominous thrum of helicopter blades. It sounded like that ghost train I often imagined I could hear, thundering its way out of the past towards me.

'They're at the farm,' Jake panted. 'I heard them getting close when I was on my bike. I was scared they'd spot me.'

When we reached Rachel I realized the vision I'd had of her as a warrior-queen was an illusion. She was as red in the face and panting as we were. Her hair was a tangled mess and her coat more shredded than ever where the brambles and thorns had snared it as she climbed.

'Are you OK?' I put my hand on her shoulder. She managed a smile.

'Just about,' she breathed.

The others had caught up by now. Jake hauled Damien up over the scrubby, stony bank and on to the line.

We stood there, gazing down the track as it curved towards the tunnel entrance.

'Come on,' Rachel said urgently and started to jog along the track, her carrier bag jostling against her thighs as she ran.

We raced after her.

Something jumped out in front of me, then dashed away, a dark shadow with a tail bobbing white until it disappeared into the gloom.

I heard Damien wail behind me. 'What was that?'

'Only a rabbit,' Rachel gasped.

'A rabbit?' Jake was dragging Damien along. 'I thought they were extinct.'

'Well, that one isn't.' I gave a silly laugh. I felt a fool I'd been scared by a rabbit. Even if I *had* never seen one before.

The tunnel entrance was completely invisible to anyone who didn't know it was there. The perfect place to hide. If you didn't know better you would just think it was a high bank overgrown with creepers. They cascaded down from the ridge above it like a waterfall of green.

Behind us the thrum . . . thrum . . . of the heli-blades was closer than ever. Damien glanced round.

'I can see them,' he squealed. 'Look!'

In the distance, the beams were searching. They had left the farm in the valley and were heading our way. We all lurched forward. Scooting along the line, Damien tripped and we hauled him to his feet. And all the time the thrum of the helicopter was getting closer . . . closer.

At the entrance we skidded to a halt. Jake hopped forward and began tearing at the climbers, pulling great lengths of it down around his feet. Behind the green jungle you could just make out the wall of plastic breeze-blocks that covered the entrance.

Rachel put her hand on his arm. 'No, Jake,' she said. 'It'll make it obvious someone's been here.'

'How else are we going to get in?' Damien said, rubbing his knee where he had fallen over.

Rachel looked at us. The moon came out from behind a cloud and I could see it reflected in her eyes. She was panting, sweating, her hair sticking to her face. 'Go now,' she said. 'Go . . . all of you. If you hurry you'll just make it back before the police arrive.'

'We can't just leave you,' I gasped.

'Yes, you can. Go!'

'You can't—' I began.

'But if we're not going to help you we needn't have come,' Damien wailed.

'You have helped me,' Rachel said. 'I wouldn't have had the courage to come here on my own. Please go.'

'But—?' I hated leaving her there. Alone, in the darkness, a strange old woman who could run like the wind.

'Please . . . ' she begged. 'Kari . . . I don't want anything to happen to you.' She gripped my arms fiercely. So fiercely I could feel her fingernails digging into my skin. 'I'll see you again, Kari.' She let go and gave me a slight push. 'Go!' she hissed. 'Now!'

I ran to catch the others up. At the top of the bank I turned to look at her. Why was she standing there watching me when she should have been desperately tying to find a way in? I had a sudden, incredible urge to go back and help her, to tear frantically at the bricks. My fingers began to throb as if I was really doing it.

But Jake was calling urgently.

'Come on, Kari.' He had scrambled down the bank and was waiting for me at the bottom.

I turned to shout to him. 'OK, I'm coming.' And when I turned back to take one last look at Rachel, she had gone.

Jake sped off in the direction of the woods as we ran indoors.

It was only minutes after we'd hurled ourselves up the stairs and into bed when the police turned up.

There was so much noise going on that none of them had noticed Damien and I had come out of our rooms and were crouching on the landing, listening.

'She's here.' I could hardly believe my ears when Dad said that in answer to their query. 'In our spare room. We've given her a bed for the night.'

'What a rotten traitor,' Damien hissed in my ear. I thumped him and told him to shut up.

The Chief, I learned later his name was Zeon, didn't seem to care that Mum had broken the law by picking Rachel up. All he wanted to do was see her and talk to her.

Mum's voice came from the front room.

'No . . . I'll get her, you'll frighten her if you just barge in.'

We dived back into our rooms and scrambled into bed. I heard Mum's footsteps go along to Rachel's room, the door open, then a gasp as she saw the empty bed. On the way back downstairs she opened my door.

'Kari . . . are you awake?'

'Yes,' I said.

'The police are here . . . they're looking for Rachel.'

'I know. I heard. Why is she so important?'

Mum came right up to the bed. I snuggled further down under the duvet hoping she wouldn't realize I'd got my outdoor clothes on. 'I don't know,' she said. 'They just said someone had reported a Drifter wandering around.'

'Oh . . . ' I supposed some people had nothing better to do.

'She's not in her room.'

'Oh?' I tried to sound innocent but I didn't know if I fooled Mum or not.

She looked at me shrewdly and was just about to say something else when heavy footsteps sounded on the stairs.

A man's voice called from the landing. 'What's the delay?'

Mum hurried out.

'I'm sorry,' I heard her say. 'She appears to have gone.'

Then the whole house exploded with running feet and shouts and angry voices and doors banging.

'Tell them to spread out,' someone shouted. 'She couldn't have gone far.'

'I'm sorry.' Dad was apologizing like mad. 'She *was* here, honestly.'

I got up then, dragged off my clothes and quickly bunged on my sleepsuit. I went out on to the landing, knuckling my eyes and pretending to have just woken up.

'What's happening?'

Chief Zeon was on the stairs, shouting something into his mobile phone. He looked at me with a dark brown stare as if I'd appeared out of the woodwork.

'My daughter, Kari,' Mum said anxiously from the hallway. 'She doesn't know anything.'

I gazed at Zeon. I could tell things about him right away. He was brimming with anxiety, an orange haze with black streaks. Real trouble. His eyes were deep set, narrow . . . shrewd eyes that told me he could suss out lies as quick as blinking.

I managed to ignore the pounding of my pulse and say 'Hi,' quite calmly as if he was making a social call.

He made Mum get Damien and they questioned us all. Damien was brilliant . . . he didn't give a thing away.

We swore we hadn't seen or heard Rachel leave. I was sure Zeon didn't believe us. But apart from using

47

torture there was nothing he could do to make us change our stories.

I went to the door with Dad to see him off. Outside was swarming with people. The road was busier than on a hot summer's day. A black truck arrived and two men with heatseekers got out. My heart sank. It was only a matter of time before they found her. But I still couldn't understand something. Why all these police just for one harmless old woman? What could she possibly have done?

5

Zeon and his men stayed outside for ages.

I didn't really understand why they hung around. The heatseekers had found Rachel in a matter of minutes. We should have known they would.

Damien and I watched miserably from the window as Zeon and the others brought her down. All our panic had been for nothing. She wasn't struggling. She was just walking between two men, calmly, upright as if they were escorting her to a meeting rather than whisking her away in a police helicopter. They helped her inside, the engine gunned, and it swept into the sky. Its winking red lights were blurred by the angry tears that were filling my eyes. I wanted to hammer on the window and yell at them to bring her back. That she was only a harmless old woman who'd lost her memory. That she wasn't a Misfit or a Drifter or any of those horrible things I'd thought she was when *I* first saw her.

But it wouldn't have done any good. They were taking her away for questioning and we would never see her again.

Later, the men with the heatseekers came down from the railway track. They chatted to the remaining patrolmen for a while. Then, one by one, they got into their vehicles and roared off into the approaching dawn. It seemed really quiet when they had gone.

'Right,' Dad said. 'That's that. Now back to bed, you kids.'

I began to shout and rant at him for giving her away. All he did was shrug and give me one of his werewolf looks. 'Did you want them turning the place upside down?' he asked. 'Much better to come out with it. I apologized on behalf of your mother.'

'Thanks,' Mum spat. She was as angry and upset as I was.

I glared at him and snorted air through my nostrils.

'Anyway . . . ' He came up close to me. 'Someone warned her they were coming, didn't they?'

I backed off, shrugging. 'She wasn't deaf . . . she must have heard them.'

'How did she know about that tunnel?' Dad asked.

I shrugged again. 'No idea.'

My brain did another blip. How *did* Rachel know about the tunnel?

But my dad didn't want to talk about it any more. He strode off towards his office, shouting over his shoulder as usual. Whenever I think of my dad I never see him face to face. Just yelling over his shoulder at one or other of us, as he heads off into his room.

'Anyway,' he hollered. 'That's *it* . . . finished. I don't want to hear you talking about her again. Do you understand? I don't know how I'm supposed to work with all this going on.'

I waited until he'd slammed his door shut before I pulled a face.

Later, when I was checking Jake got home safely, I told him all about it.

'Why didn't she tell us the police were after her? We wouldn't have given her away,' he said. He still looked flushed from his mad bike ride through the woods to avoid the police in the roadway.

'I don't know,' I said. 'And now we probably *never* will.'

Then I asked him if he'd noticed anything strange about the police.

'No,' he said. 'I was too scared to notice anything really.'

'Well, they weren't *ordinary* police, were they?'

He shrugged. 'They weren't in uniform.'

'No,' I said. 'It wasn't that. They weren't interested in anything but Rachel. Zeon couldn't have cared less about Mum breaking the law, he just wanted Rachel, that's all.'

Jake frowned. 'Yeah, I guess you're right.'

'And he didn't have the air of a policeman . . . he was too het up . . . too worried about just catching up with some raggy old woman. It was almost as if it was the most important thing in the universe.'

Jake was looking puzzled. 'They just seemed like regular guys doing their job to me.'

But nothing would convince me I was wrong. There was something about Zeon I couldn't quite fathom out. And I still felt miserable about letting Rachel down.

'There's nothing more we could have done,' Jake said, trying to cheer me up.

'No,' I said, grey with misery. 'I suppose not. Where do you think they'll take her?'

He shook his head. 'No idea. Loony bin or old people's home, I suppose.'

'I'm going back to the tunnel,' I told him. 'She might have left something behind.'

'What kind of thing?'

I shrugged. 'I don't know. I just want to go and look.'

'OK,' Jake grinned. 'Wait for me.' The screen went blank.

I hadn't seen my dad that morning. In fact I didn't think I ever wanted to see him again.

I went outside and waited for Jake to turn up. It was a bright, yellow morning that didn't match my mood at all.

It was oddly quiet by the tunnel entrance. Not even the hum of the city reached us on the early morning air. All I *could* hear was the breathing of the wind through the grasses then a sudden rush of sound as a wave of birds flew overhead. There were a few cars going up and down the road, stopping to stare at the Cottage then going on their way. The people driving didn't seem to notice us scrambling up the bank and disappearing over the top to chase along the railway line.

Jake hopped forward and pulled back some of the creeper.

'Wow!' Then he said in a kind of strangled voice that sounded as if it came from someone else, 'Hey, Kari . . . come and look at this.'

It was a hole. Big enough for you to climb through. The jagged edges were burned, scarred. It looked as if the bricks had been blasted away by a bomb.

I put my head inside and stared into the gloom. I could make out loads of stuff littering the floor. Debris . . . old bottles, cans, rags, paper . . . blocks, some shattered into fragments. The relics of a bygone age—just as I'd imagined.

I wrinkled my nose. There was a smell . . . smells. Stuffiness, decay, the acid smell of damp earth. And something else . . . something burnt. Maybe it was fumes from those ghost trains I used to think I could hear.

'Yuk,' I breathed. 'It stinks.' My voice echoed. Stinks . . . stinks . . . stinks . . . stinks . . . stinks . . . it bounced back at me.

Jake was looking around outside with a frown on his face.

'How could she have done it?'

I knew his mind was ticking over. All those science files he'd accessed and studied. All those projects he'd done. But this one had him really puzzled.

'She couldn't have,' I said. 'It must have been here before.'

'I'm going in to have a look,' he said. 'Coming?'

'Sure.' I sounded braver than I felt.

As soon as I got inside an ominous black feeling swept over me. All the ghosts came crowding in. I imagined I could hear voices, the rattle of machinery, brightness at the other end where sunlight must have once streamed

52

in. Through it, huge figures walking around like they had in my dream. I had imagined it so often it seemed almost familiar. As if I had been there before in some other life.

Jake was examining the inside of the hole. 'Definitely an explosive of some kind,' he sniffed one of the bricks and muttered to himself. 'Maybe she found something. You know, something left from years ago.'

'People didn't leave explosives around then any more than they do now,' I said scornfully. I had managed to shake off the ghosts and was standing beside him, ankle deep in garbage. 'Anyway it wouldn't be any good after all these years.'

Jake took off his baseball cap and ran his hand over his hair. 'I dunno, then,' he said. 'I just don't know.'

Suddenly I spied something . . . Rachel's coat. The police must have just thought it was a bundle of rags.

I ran and picked it up. I felt through one of the pockets and pulled out a piece of paper with something written on it. I stuck it into the back pocket of my jeans to look at later.

I felt in the other pocket. Amidst screwed-up tissues my fingers closed over something cold. I knew straight away what it was. Rachel's bracelet.

'Oh, wow!' Jake said when I drew it out. 'Fancy leaving that behind. Do you think she meant to?'

'I don't know.' I stuck it into my pocket. 'Come on.' I suddenly wanted to get out in the air. 'This place gives me the creeps.'

As we turned to go I spotted something else lying amongst the stuff on the floor. I picked it up. 'Look, Jake.'

It was a doll. A plastic one, soft and pliable with a dirty baby face. Its curly blonde hair was green with mould and its little pink sleepsuit filthy with damp and dirt. Clutching it, feeling it, gave me a strange sensation . . . I was a little kid again . . . three, maybe four years old.

'Poor thing,' I said. 'I wonder how it got here?'

Jake was giving me a weird look. 'Your mum told me you hated dolls.'

I went on staring at it, feeling its soft arms and legs.

'Did she?' I said. 'Maybe that's why she never bought me one.'

I lifted my arm to chuck it away but something stopped me. Instead, I tucked it inside my jacket. 'Come on,' I said. 'Let's go.'

'Well,' Jake said as we made our way back to the house. 'That's it then. We'll never know who she was or where she came from.'

'No,' I said sadly.

But thoughts were chasing one another wildly round in my head. *I'll see you again* . . . Rachel's words echoed in my brain . . . *I'll see you again.*

And, strangely, I couldn't get rid of the certainty that one day I really would.

When we got indoors there was a message from Vinny.

> When can I come to see you? I'm dying to get out of the suburbs—it's so hot and stuffy and the air is foul this week. :-)

I e-mailed her back.

> We'll fix something soon.

I could have got her on the videophone but I didn't really feel like talking just then. All I could think about was Rachel.

Jake was sprawled on my bed and lay looking up at the ceiling. He'd said the patterns looked as if they should tell some kind of story and I guessed he was trying to figure out what.

I took the dirty old doll from my coat and stuck it away in a drawer. I didn't know why but for some reason I couldn't bear to throw it away.

I laid out the stuff I'd found in Rachel's pockets. The screwed up paper . . . the bracelet. I flattened out the paper. What I saw made me draw in my breath. It was a musical score.

Jake was staring at it.

'Play it,' he said.

I went to my machine and keyed it in. It came back to me within micro-seconds . . . the same haunting melody I'd heard from the piano the night we had been talking out in the garden. It had been Rachel playing it, not Mum.

I played it several times then went to get my flute. It sounded good on that too, a sort of beige, calm melody that gave you a feeling of peace and contentment.

'Do you recognize it?' Jake asked.

I shook my head. 'No.'

'That's all the answers we're getting,' he said.

I frowned 'What do you mean?'

'No,' he said. 'No, no. Do we know who Rachel is or where she came from? No. Do we know why Zeon's monkeys were after her? No. Do we know where they've taken her—'

'OK, OK,' I interrupted. 'You've made your point.'

I went to my drawer and took out the doll. I laid it on the bed. It gave me a uncanny sensation seeing it beside Rachel's bracelet. A feeling that they were both part of a strange puzzle. And that when I'd managed to fit them together I would understand what had happened to change my life for ever.

'Hey.' Jake sat up rapidly and picked the bracelet up. He peered at the engraving. 'That's really weird.'

'What?'

He held it up to the light. 'A website address . . . look . . . '

And there it was, engraved on the solid piece in the

centre of the chain. Why I hadn't realized what it was before I'd never know.

Ra@starhost.dck/Cty.uk

Jake went to sit in front of my machine and clicked on the mail facility.

'What are you doing?'

'Sending a message,' he said. 'What do you think?'

I stood beside him, peering eagerly at the screen. Rachel wouldn't be there. She was probably holed up in some horrible police cell or had been carted off to a home. But someone might be . . . someone who knew her. It could be the address of the friends she told me she'd got in the City.

My heart was thudding loudly. Maybe at last we'd solve *some* of the puzzle.

But the screen came up *'site unavailable'*.

'Sorry,' Jake shrugged. 'We need a password. We'll never work out what in a hundred years. We'll try again later and see what happens.'

So we did. We tried loads of times but the same message came up again and again.

I sat on the bed feeling grey again. I held the bracelet in my hand. It lay cool against the skin of my palm.

'She meant us to find this, I'm sure,' I said to Jake. 'She wouldn't have just simply forgotten it.' I told him how she fingered it all the time as if she was making sure she hadn't lost it. 'It's a City address and she told me she would head for the City.'

Jake was biting his lip. 'I *could* try to find out exactly where it is.'

Jake was a whizz at hacking into Netfiles where he had no right to be.

I felt better all of a sudden. 'Go on, then,' I urged. 'Do it now.'

First he accessed Peoplefinder and searched a database of millions of addresses. No luck. He tried another directory but they weren't in there either.

An hour later he came up with something. I'd almost

given up and was sitting by the window gazing out at the string of tourists who had decided to leave their cars on the verge and take a stroll down the road.

'Docklands!' Jake's voice smashed in on daydreams.

I turned swiftly. 'Docklands!' My heart bungey-jumped. Docklands was definitely a no-go area. Derelict and dangerous. Home to crimmos, drug barons, gangsters, terrorists, and Misfits. Why Rachel's friends' Website address was there I had no idea. No one with an ounce of self-preservation went near.

Jake sat back with a sigh. 'That's all we're going to get, I'm afraid. *Starhost* doesn't throw anything up at all.'

'It'll be a start,' I said.

He gazed at me suspiciously. 'What do you mean?'

'I'm going to try to find it.'

'I've been trying for the last hour.'

'No, stupid,' I said. 'I'm going to the City.'

Jake stared at me in horror. 'You're joking.'

I shook my head. 'I'm deadly serious. She wants me to. I'm going, Jake.'

I didn't even really know why I was saying it. All I knew was that I had to help her. If I found her friends and told them what had happened they might be able to vouch for her . . . get her away from the police. It was just something I knew I *had* to do.

Jake got hold of my arms. 'You're crazy, Kari.' He shook his head. 'It could be an old address, deleted years ago. She could have found the bracelet somewhere . . . you can't go there, Kari, you're crazy.'

'I know but I'm going anyway.'

Jake shook his head. 'I don't think I'll ever understand you in a million years,' he said.

I flashed him a sad grin. 'Wish me luck.'

'Don't be daft,' he said. 'I'm coming with you.'

'No . . . your mum?'

'If you go on your own you're dead, Kari. You'll need help and I'm the one to do it.'

I grinned. Then an idea flashed into my head. 'We could say we're visiting Vinny.'

'Anything,' he said. 'As long as no one starts sending out search parties for us.'

'She'll cover us. I know she will,' I said.

'OK, then . . . get her.'

I keyed her number in and got her straight away. She looked great. I had never seen her face-to-face but on screen she was really pretty. Last winter I'd answered a message on the Net saying she wanted a friend in the country and we'd been buddies ever since.

'Kari!' She was grinning all over her face. She'd got her hair dyed purple and plaited all round her head with orange beads at the end of each one. She'd had her nose pierced since I talked to her last. 'I got your message. Is this the *soon* you were on about? You don't hang about, do you?'

'Er . . . no.' I went on to explain.

'The City!' she breathed. 'Wow . . . on your own?'

'Me and Jake. We fancied a bit of excitement. It's really boring out here.' I didn't dare tell her the truth.

She pulled a face. 'Well, OK, you can say you're visiting my place if you like. My dad's abroad so there's no one here to give you away.'

'Thanks, Vinny. I expect Mum will contact you just to make sure it's OK.'

'No problem,' Vinny said. 'I'll know what to say.'

As I logged off, my heart drummed . . . fear . . . excitement . . . everything.

We were going to the City . . . the City . . . the City . . .

PART TWO

In the City

6

Harsh, savage rock music blared out from Razz's blaster. The heavy stuff he was mad about.

He lay under his thin blankets, his whole body moving in time to the frantic drum rhythm. He was in another world. Lost . . . his heart thudding a wild and crazy beat.

When the track finished he came to. He stretched out his arm and switched the radio off. With a groan he rolled off the mattress and padded across the bare floor to the window. He tugged aside the rough bit of sacking that covered the broken glass. He yawned and stretched his arms above his head. The smell of the river rose on the hot, heavy air. A dark, muddy, garbage kind of smell. There was a barge going past, ploughing its way through the murky water towards the wharf. It was loaded with boxes. To the east, the sun was rising, colourwashing the heavy cloud of pollution a dull, blood red. The towers and spires of the City were carved darkly against a backdrop of crimson.

Razz hurried into the washroom. If you didn't get to the wharf early there was no chance of getting any goods to sell. He cupped his hands under the cold, rusty water that trickled constantly from the broken tap. He rinsed his face quickly, then rubbed his teeth with his index finger. He peered into the jagged fragment that served as a mirror, combed his fingers through his long curly hair then tied it back with an old leather bootlace he'd found yesterday when he was helping out on Swampy's stall. Then he went to the loose floorboard where he kept his

61

Euros. Took out a wad, packed it into the inside pocket of his jacket and zipped it up. Then he grabbed his skateboard, shoved it under his arm and ran out, racing down the twelve flights of stairs, two at a time. At the bottom he grabbed the tatty kid's buggy he used as a cart and headed for the front door.

Outside, he almost collided with a couple of lost looking Strangers.

'Sorry.' The girl looked about his age. She had clean hair down to her waist. It was a colour he'd never seen before. Rusty red, like the sky had been that morning and brushed to a perfect shine. She'd got pearly skin, a freckled snub nose, green eyes and a little, pointy chin like a picture of an elf he'd seen in a book once. He stared at her quickly then dropped his glance. She was staring at *him* and it gave him a funny feeling. As if she could see right into his head.

'Watch it!' he growled. He jumped on his board and scooted off, dragging the cart behind him. He felt her watching but didn't turn. Her companion hadn't said a word. Only her name shouted in warning as Razz had almost hurtled into her.

'Kari!' He'd grabbed her arm and pulled her out of the way.

Razz noticed their clothes and grinned to himself. Smart sportsuits, chunky trainers, each carried a bright coloured ruckbag. They must really be stupid coming here dressed like that. They stuck out like a couple of sore thumbs. Those clothes, the ruckbags . . . they'd be off their backs in no time if they didn't watch out. What a couple like them were doing around here he'd got no idea. Lost probably. Strangers never came here on purpose.

There was already a queue at the wharf.

'Oi, don't you push in!' A woman with a sticky-faced child in a grimy buggy shouted at Razz as he skidded to a halt. He had no intention of pushing in. It was more than his life was worth. The woman might look harmless enough but she might be one of the Baron's spies for all he knew.

'Sorry, lady,' he mumbled. He cast his eyes down. It always worked. No eye-contact, no challenge. People he didn't know thought he was pretty brainless and that was exactly what he wanted them to think. Most people his age went around in gangs. Not Razz. Being on his own was just the way he liked it.

He picked up his board and tucked it under his arm. He craned his neck. The bargemaster was unloading the stuff on to the quay. His two burly mates were keeping the people back until he was ready to barter.

Razz got a box of software. *Timescan* was written on the front. Great! It had cost him an arm and a leg but he should be able to sell it for double. Grinning inanely at everyone he pushed his way through the crowd and headed back home. Once he'd got it sorted he knew *just* the place to flog it, the place where he'd get most money.

'Hey, Razzle-Dazzle!' Swampy called out as Razz shot through the market.

Razz ground to a halt. He grinned. Swampy was the only one who called him Razzle-Dazzle these days. He'd got the nickname when he was small because he loved picking up old bits of jewellery, sequins, glass beads . . . anything colourful that caught the light. He fixed them on his clothes, his boots, skateboard . . . anywhere they would go. He'd grown out of the craze now but the nickname had stuck.

Swampy had fresh fruit on his stall today. He'd been up long before dawn to meet the first barge that chugged downriver. He had been Razz's friend for as long as Razz could remember. Swampy had been all over the World before he fell foul of the law and ended up here. Razz loved listening to his travelling tales.

He looked longingly at Swampy's fruit. 'Save me some of them oranges, huh?' His mouth watered at the thought.

Swampy was just fixing on his cash belt. 'Let's see the colour of yer money.' He grinned as Razz shot off.

'Later,' Razz shouted over his shoulder.

Back in the skyblock a couple of Addicts had blundered into the lobby and were lying amongst the rubbish at the bottom of the stairs. Razz hung on to his box for grim death as he stepped over them and ran up the stairs. He heard one call out but ignored her. His heart was thumping like one of those crazy drum solos he was mad on. He'd got a feeling it was going to be a great day and no one was going to spoil it. He dived into his room, slammed the door and fixed the makeshift bar across. The Addicts weren't likely to make it this far up but you couldn't be too careful.

He sat on the floor and began to sort the stuff out. There was a corporation over at the Pool who'd kill for it. He had no idea what kind of operation they were running there and he didn't really care. He might even get enough Euros to buy one of those sportsuits like those Strangers were wearing. If he saw them again he'd ask them where they got them. He might even try to get up Westend if he felt rich . . . and reckless.

By the time he'd got the stuff sorted Razz was starving. He stopped off at the burger stall.

'Any meat today?' he asked Vi.

She wiped her hands on her greasy apron and shook her head. 'Veggie.'

Razz shrugged. 'OK.' He gave her all his loose change. 'That's all I've got.'

Vi knew him too well. 'Yeah, I bet.'

Luckily she had a soft spot for him. He'd even dossed down at her place for a while when he was younger. He ran errands for Vi, taking goods here and there, picking up parcels. He never knew what was in them and was sensible enough never to ask.

Vi was grinning at him as she handed him the burger. 'Enjoy,' she said.

'Ta.' He picked up the squeezy bottle and covered the burger with ketchup.

Vi leaned her huge bulk over the van's counter and peered at his cart. 'What you got today?'

'Nothing much,' he fibbed.

She wrinkled her nose. 'No good to me if you can't eat it.'

He grinned and waved. 'See yer, Vi.'

He went along the river road. It was safer there with buildings only on one side. Quiet too. It must have been the heat keeping people off the streets. It rose in a shimmer from the wharfsides, from the abandoned cars, even from the piles of rat-infested rubbish littering the road. There were the usual Misfits hanging around but they didn't bother him. One group had lit a fire in an old oil drum and were dancing around it hooting and hollering as if they were doing a war dance. He kept his head down and gave them a wide berth.

It took him over an hour to reach the Pool. He scooted past the once-posh apartment blocks. Vandalized now. Their gaping windows were like nostrils breathing in the desolation. Three barricades to climb, dodging around patrols, stopping once to stare at a flock of seagulls squabbling over the unrecognizable carcass of a dead animal.

When he got there the place was totally deserted. Piles of garbage, the remains of bonfires were evidence that it had been the haunt of Misfits and Drifters. But it looked as if they'd moved on. Razz stood for a minute or two, looking . . . listening . . . He shuddered. The place really gave him the creeps. It seemed full of ghost-echoes, of the voices of the past. He liked real noise, engines, people, music, the hoots of the water traffic. The only sounds here were made by the wind as it whined through the broken windows and rattled the hanging slats of the blinds. Grass and weeds grew everywhere, through paving slabs, up the sides of buildings. There was even a tree growing through one of the shattered window-frames. Razz wondered how it had managed to take root and thrive in a place like this. He supposed it was a bit like himself. Scraping a living from whatever it could. But why the corporation chose to be right out here he'd got no idea. He'd only been here a couple of times before. Once when he'd got some hardware to flog and someone had told him they'd heard a new corporation was setting up here.

The other . . . He didn't really like to think about it. The only thing worth remembering was that he'd managed to escape through one of the old deserted waterhouses and had lost the muggers in the maze of underground tunnels. In fact, he'd got lost himself. He'd been so shattered he'd stayed down there all night. Then he'd been scared by nightmares . . . lights shining, people coming towards him.

He hadn't been able to get out fast enough.

He skirted the bombed glass towerblock and dodged into one of the narrow alleyways that led to the square. Someone had made a ramshackle shelter of wood and old tarpaulins but when he looked in it was empty except for a pile of used hypos, empty beer cans, and a few discarded bottles. A rat scurried out as he kicked it down and hoisted his cart across the debris. There was a skip at the end of the alley full of bits of timber and old roofing material, old computers and polybags. Razz ducked down and peered round it, making sure it was safe to go on.

A couple of mangy black dogs were sniffing round the base of the derelict fountain. Razz waited a minute or two then walked out into the open. He whistled. They loped towards him, ears back, tails wagging cautiously. He fed them the bits of burger bun he'd saved in case he met any. They jumped up, fawning for more.

'Sorry, mates . . . ' He spread his hands to show they were empty. He wanted to stroke them, to fondle their rough fur but they lost interest and ambled away.

66

He looked around. This place was mega-creepy. Haunted. He'd heard someone had seen ghosts out here. Phantoms that drifted out of nowhere. There had been a slaughterhouse near here years ago. Maybe they had been terrified ghost-animals haunting the place where they had met their death.

He sat down on the wall tapping his heels against it impatiently. Last time, someone had spotted him and had suddenly appeared from a doorway. He remembered he'd almost jumped out of his skin. He shivered suddenly. He could feel someone, somewhere, watching him. Maybe it was one of those ghosts? He peered upwards, squinting, but couldn't see a soul.

Then, suddenly, he heard something. Music. He whirled, almost upsetting the cart. He strained his ears. A frown knotted his brows. It seemed to be all around, echoing, bouncing off the walls, ringing through the sightless windows, spiralling up into the sky. He drew in his breath, still wheeling, still trying to locate its source.

Then it stopped. Someone had switched it off. The silence caught him unawares and he sat down heavily on the fountain wall. He found himself wishing it would start up again. It wasn't the crazy metal stuff he usually liked. This had been tame in comparison. But the strings . . . the percussion . . . They had made his senses reel.

Then he heard a voice and a man suddenly appeared from one of the doorways.

'Hey . . . Razz, isn't it?' he called.

Razz sprang to his feet as if he'd been shot. The cart twisted and turned and the boxes fell, scattering themselves in little heaps over the cobblestones. He dived to gather them up, holding them against his chest, scared the man might grab them from him. When he got to his feet the man was standing in front of him.

'Hey,' he said again. 'Let me help.'

Razz dodged back away from the outstretched hand.

'It's OK. I'm not going to take them from you. I just wanted to help.'

'Sorry,' Razz mumbled. He looked the man in the eye. He realized it was the same one he'd dealt with before. Tall with blond hair. Amazing, turbulent blue eyes: a jaw that looked as if it had been chiselled from concrete. A dead ringer for a movie star.

Razz relaxed as much as he dared.

The man crouched beside him. 'Are those for us?'

'Er . . . yeah, if you can pay,' Razz said. He piled the stuff back into the buggy.

'Of course we can pay. Do you want to come up and we'll sort something out?'

They both stood up.

'Come up?' Razz said. Last time they'd done the deal in the square. He hadn't trusted the man enough to go indoors with him. After they'd struck a bargain he had shot off as fast as he could. He swallowed nervously. He wanted to go inside with him but he was scared stiff.

The man put a hand on his arm. Razz flinched and took a step backwards. His heart thudded. His eyes darted one way, then the other. There were plenty of places he could run to but would he be fast enough? This guy looked pretty fit.

The man obviously sensed his fear. 'Look,' he said gently. 'My name's Jon. You've got nothing to be scared of.'

Gently but insistently he propelled Razz towards one of the buildings. At the door he keyed in a code and a voice came through the speaker. The voice said something in a foreign language and Jon answered.

The doorlock clicked and Jon pushed it open. Razz hung back, still uncertain.

'It's OK,' Jon said. 'Honestly.'

It was on the tip of Razz's tongue to say he wasn't scared. But he'd got the feeling Jon would know it was a lie.

Inside was like nothing in the World. Razz's jaw fell open as he looked around. Carpeted stairs, shiny stainless steel walls and handrails. Jon held his arm as they went up.

At the top, Razz hung back, dazzled by bright lights. He was trying to take it all in but was having trouble believing what he saw.

'Come on,' Jon insisted. 'This way.'

There was a sign on the door. *Starhost*. Then a line of odd looking symbols in blues, greens, yellows, reds . . . patterns that seemed to whirl and dance before his eyes.

At last Razz found his voice.

'What is this place?' he said. His voice sounded croaky. He cleared his throat. 'Who done it up?'

'We did.' Jon pushed open the door. Razz dragged the cart through. The brightness dazzled him again. Music echoed softly in the background. There were flowers in a vase on the window shelf. The sweet scent hit his nostrils and almost sent him reeling backwards. It was all so strange, so alien and Razz was suddenly so scared he wanted to run . . . dive down the stairs, across the square . . . back home. He suddenly didn't care about the goods . . . the money. He just wanted out.

'Mal,' Jon was saying to the woman behind the desk. 'This is Razz, he's brought us some software.'

'Great.' She gazed at Razz. Her stare was so frankly curious he felt colour come to his cheeks.

After they'd done the deal, Jon said, 'Would you like to look round?'

Razz fingered the wad of Euros in his pocket. The sooner he got home and stashed it, the better. There was enough to get that sportsuit, batteries for his radio, maybe even some second-hand boots . . . some with the flashers in the heels like he had always wanted. It would be better to get going before they changed their minds about being so generous.

But curiosity got the better of him.

'Er . . . yeah,' he said. 'OK.'

On his way back he realized he never had found out exactly what they did. His tour round had dazzled him

69

so much he'd hardly taken anything in. It had been almost like visiting another planet.

Computers . . . loads of them . . . all working. People sitting around in groups. The operators stopped tapping away on their keyboards to stare at him with a kind of grave curiosity. Blood pounded in his temples as they shook his hand. Some asked him where he lived . . . if he had any brothers and sisters. He'd told them he didn't really live anywhere and he didn't know if he had any brothers and sisters or not.

He wanted to ask them questions too. Where *they* lived, how they managed to get there every day when the light railway had been bombed years ago, the tunnel abandoned, and the roads barricaded ever since he could remember. Maybe they were like him and skated or walked although somehow he doubted it. Anyway, asking questions was dangerous so instead he just took it all in, tried to stamp it on his brain so when he was back in his dismal room he could drag it out and relive it over again.

Jon went with him down the stairs.

'Let us know if you get any more . . . goods.'

'Yeah.' Razz still felt bewildered by his experience. He was still wondering what was in the rooms that Jon hadn't shown him.

'We know the journey here's dangerous for you,' Jon went on.

Razz shrugged. 'There's worse.'

'Yes,' Jon said. 'I'm sure. But perhaps you could mail me next time and let us know. It might save you the journey if it's stuff we've already got.'

'Yeah?' Razz's mind raced. It was really hard to get access to a machine but if he had a few spare Euros he might be able to bribe someone. And he'd really like to see Jon again. 'Give me your address then,' he said.

Jon took a notebook from his pocket, wrote down the site address and tore it out. Razz shoved it into the back pocket of his jeans. 'Ta.'

Before he left Jon said something else. 'It would be better not to say you'd been here or give anyone our address.'

Razz shot him a grin. 'Don't be daft,' he said. 'A dealer would be nuts to give away his customers.' They wouldn't believe me anyway, he added to himself.

Jon looked up at the darkening sky. 'Will you be all right?'

'All right?' Razz realized Jon had said that because it was almost night. He had been there longer than he realized. 'Yeah, I'll be all right,' he said. 'I'm not scared of the dark.'

He knew Jon was watching as he skirted the fountain, scooted along towards the alley, and made his way back towards the waterfront. If he was lucky he might be able to hop on a passing barge and avoid the long trek back. He could hole up somewhere until morning but he'd rather get back and stash away his wad.

At the entrance to the alley Razz turned to see if Jon was still watching but he had gone. He sighed, thinking of all the things he'd seen. How great it would be to work in a place like that. In a room where music played . . . whatever kind of stuff that got you going. If he had ever really thought what a heaven would be like, that would definitely be it.

He stood for a while at the top of the river Stairs. There was an old motor cruiser moored up at the bottom. It didn't look as if it had been used for years. A stiff breeze had sprung up and the water lapped noisily against its hull.

On the opposite bank, lights were coming on. They were reflected in the water, shimmering, moving like a mobile city of stars. The derelict cranes were huge skeletal fretworks against the darkening sky. One had toppled over, crashing into one of the old wharves where it lay twisted and bent like a felled dinosaur.

Razz felt in his back pocket and pulled out the piece of paper Jon had given him.

71

Ra@starhost.dck/Cty.uk.

He stared at it for a minute or two, memorizing it. Then a sudden gust ripped it from his fingers and hurled it out into the middle of the river where it fell and floated along with the current like a little white sailing boat.

Razz watched it until it disappeared beneath the black water.

Ra@starhost.dck/Cty.uk.

He knew he wouldn't forget it.

He gazed downriver towards the bridge but there were no barges in sight. He sighed and began to make his way home.

7

The building was in darkness when Razz reached his skyblock. Street level lights illuminated the lobby, sending sparks into the empty cans and bottles and casting shadows into the gloom of the stairwell. There was always something reassuring about those piles of rubbish. It meant that no one wanted to claim the building and clean it up. If the Baron and his disciples decided to take it over that would be that. Razz and all the other inhabitants would be out . . . or dead. There would be no way they could afford to pay protection.

He left his cart inside the broken lift and ran up the stairs, two at a time. He still felt great . . . all that money. He would go out later and get a proper meal somewhere. Not flash it around, of course. Just take a few notes. His mouth watered. He was still starving. He never had gone back for those oranges.

Razz's good mood evaporated when he got to his floor. The door to his room had been kicked in, smashed to smithereens. Inside, someone had slashed his mattress and scattered his clothes all over the place. His saucepans were gone, his stashed tins of food, his little stove, his things from the washroom. He ran his hand through his hair and groaned. He went into the little room adjoining the one where he slept. He groaned again. Gone. His precious drum set he'd risked life and limb to get out of a skip near Green Witches bridge. He felt a red haze of anger rise in front of his eyes. He went over, bent to pick something up. One lousy drumstick was all they'd left him. Angrily he put it over his knee, cracked it in two, and hurled the pieces out of the window.

Breathing heavily, he went back into the other room, across to the filing cabinet pushed up against one wall. He grunted as he put his shoulder to it and heaved. Then he gave a sigh of relief. At least they hadn't got his radio. He'd have gone bonkers if they'd taken that too. He reached behind and pulled it out. Then he patted his pocket reassuringly. He'd got his wad, his skateboard, his radio . . . downstairs, his cart. It was obviously time to move on. Maybe Vi would give him a mattress for the night if he was lucky. Maybe, one day, he'd get some more drums.

He was just about to leave when he heard a noise. A shuffle, a whisper . . . coming from the room across the corridor. He froze. As far as he knew, the place was totally rubbished, uninhabitable. Maybe those Addicts had got up here after all? It had probably been them who trashed his room. They must have been livid when they didn't find any stuff. Perhaps they were lying in wait for him to go back down the stairs?

Words shot into his brain. Fight or flight. There was nothing here to fight for so he'd better scarper. Quick. Before they came out of hiding and decided to slash him as well as his mattress.

He was just about to dive along the corridor when he caught sight of something that stopped him in his tracks. Outside, the heli-patrol was hammering its way across the rooftops. The laserlight shone into the windows. Its beam caught something. A flash of red, a pale face, wide, scared eyes blinking in the sudden, blinding light. Razz knew at once it wasn't Addicts who were holed up in there, it was the Strangers he'd seen earlier. He felt a surge of curiosity and, strangely, pity.

The helicopter drummed away and the room was plunged again into darkness.

Razz stood in the doorway, his board under his arm. He gave his eyes time to get used to the gloom. He could just make out two figures crouched in a corner. He swallowed. He could be wrong and it wasn't them at all.

Recklessly, he took a chance.

'You lost?' he asked.

He saw the girl glance at the boy. Then they both stood up and stepped cautiously away from the corner and came towards him. They held hands.

The boy spoke. His voice was croaky and didn't seem to come out right. So he cleared his throat and started again.

'Yeah,' he said. 'I don't suppose you'd be able to help us, would you?'

Razz leaned against the door frame. 'Cost you,' he said.

The girl came forward. She was fumbling in her ruckbag, searching for something. A purse . . . a knife . . . a gun?

Razz dodged back then let out his breath when she took out a flashlight and clicked it on. She shone it full into his face. He put his hand over his eyes.

'Hey, watch it.'

'Sorry.' She lowered the beam. 'We haven't got any money,' she said in a small voice. 'We lost it.'

'Had it pinched,' the boy said.

'Yes,' she said. 'We got mugged. And then we got hopelessly lost. We must have been going round in circles because we ended up here again.'

She placed the torch upright on the floor. Razz could see them properly now. They weren't wearing their flash clothes any more. She had on a ragged pair of jeans, an old, stained leather jacket with fringes dangling from the sleeves. He was wearing tatty grey jogging pants and a black T-shirt with half a picture of a naked skull on the front. The rest was covered in white paint or something. One sleeve was almost torn off. It was pretty obvious the stuff came from a skip.

The girl must have seen him looking. She stared down at herself. 'We sold our sportsuits and our shoes and mobile phones and our pocket PCs,' she said. 'But we had that money pinched too.'

With a quick flick of her head she flung her hair back over her shoulder. Then she grinned suddenly, broadly, and it was as if the sun had come out.

'Couple of twits, me and Jake,' she said.

Razz relaxed and grinned back. 'Not 'arf.'

Kari held up her arm. 'At least I've managed to keep these.' Metal bracelets rattled on her wrist as she tucked another stray lock of hair behind her ear. Slotted in between the bracelets was a different one. One made of a bright material he'd never seen before. He thought how lucky she'd been. He knew of people who'd cut someone's arm off to get at their jewellery.

She came towards him. He felt a strange sensation. He wanted to reach out and touch the redness of her hair. Put his fingers round her bony wrist and pull her closer. He stopped himself just in time. She was scared . . . of him, of the building, the night . . . everything. She was putting on a brave face but she was frightened silly. When he'd first seen her he'd thought she could see into his mind. Now, he could see into hers. She had an air about her. Not only fear but a determination to overcome it. He could always tell that kind of thing. She had tilted her head to one side and was staring into his eyes.

'Where do you come from?' he asked.

She glanced at Jake again. 'The country,' she said.

Razz snorted. 'The country?' He was surprised. He'd thought they were Westenders. 'You're crazy . . . coming 'ere.'

'We're looking for someone,' Jake said. 'Do you think you could help?'

Razz noticed suddenly that the girl was shaking. She'd stuffed her hands into the pocket of her jacket but couldn't stop them trembling. Jake was hugging himself for warmth. Even in the hot weather this building was cold.

Razz shrugged. 'If you ain't got no Euros . . . '

'You could have my ruckbag,' Kari said eagerly. She eyed his board and his radio. 'You could put your things in it.'

'They wouldn't fit.' He sneered even though his mouth almost watered at the thought of carrying a bag like that.

'Well . . . ' She shrugged her shoulders. 'Your clothes and stuff.'

'I ain't got any . . . ' Razz looked down at himself. 'Only these.'

'We could send you some Euros when we get back home,' Jake said.

'You mean *if* you get back,' Razz said.

'Yeah, well . . . ' Jake shrugged and raised his eyebrows.

Then Kari did something that caught Razz unawares. She came right up to him and put her hand on his arm. Through the material of his jacket he could feel how cold her fingers were.

He tensed, then relaxed when she smiled up at him.

'Please,' she said. 'What's your name?'

He told her, clearing his throat.

'Razz . . . ' She said it as if she'd never heard the word before. She made it sound different, almost musical. She lengthened the zzzz and made it sound like the gentle buzzing of a bee. 'If we could just ask you something then we'll go, honestly. And if you leave your address we'll send you some—'

'Address?' he said. He looked around, glancing back into his trashed room. 'I ain't got no address.'

The two Strangers exchanged glances again. Their look said it all. Confusion, anxiety, fear . . . Razz made a sudden decision. He *would* help them if he could. In spite of his room being rubbished he still felt good with all that money stashed in his pockets. It wouldn't hurt to do what these guys wanted. Especially if they could pay.

'OK,' he said reluctantly. 'What do yer want to know?'

Kari smiled again. Her teeth were white . . . even . . . perfect. Her fingers tightened on his sleeve. Even though they were cold, he felt a strange warmth snake all the way up his arm and invade his heart.

'Oh, thanks, Razz.' She shivered and stuffed her other hand back in her pocket. 'I don't suppose you could lend us the money for a cup of tea, first, could you?'

He took them to the café under the old railway arches. He decided he must be crazy, spending his hard-earned Euros on two complete Strangers.

Pad, the island man, was serving behind the counter. The small room was thick with smoke and the smell of grease from frying chips. Going in, Kari put her hand over her mouth.

'What's up?' Razz gazed at her.

'Er . . . nothing.' She managed a wry grin.

There was an empty table in the corner by the juke box. Jake stared at it curiously. Feeling generous, Razz took a coin out of his pocket.

''ere.' He handed it, rough with embarrassment, to Jake. 'Put something on if you want.'

He got them meat sandwiches and huge mugs of tea so strong you could dye your hair with it. Kari stared at the thick wodges of bread dripping with grease. She swallowed then smiled at him.

'Thanks.' She clasped her hands round the mug to draw in its warmth. Jake was still trying to choose what disc to play.

'I don't know any of that stuff.' He sat down and took a gulp of tea.

'It's all pretty old,' Razz told them.

Then the machine clicked and Jake's choice began to play. An old rock number that was a hit years and years ago.

Kari was tucking in to her sandwich as if she hadn't eaten for a month.

Razz couldn't take his eyes off her. The heat from the crowded room had washed colour into her cheeks. She had tucked her hair behind her ears although it kept falling forward again. She wore tiny ear-rings, sparkling diamonds against the paleness of her skin. He almost gave in to the incredible urge to touch her hair. Just to find out what it felt like, to rub it between his fingers. He thought of his own hair, wild and tangled, scraped back, dirty. Maybe he'd spend a few precious Euros on a bath.

When Kari had finished eating she explained why they'd come to the City and who they were looking for.

'We're frightened they've locked Rachel up some-where,' she said breathlessly. 'So if we can locate her friends they might be able to help her.'

Then Jake butted in.

'The thing is,' he said. 'They weren't *ordinary* police that tracked her down and to be honest we're not sure *what* they're going to do with her.'

'Or why they were so keen to find her,' Kari added. 'They brought a heli-patrol, heatseekers . . . everything.' She gave a shudder as if the memory scared her.

Razz shook his head, confused by the whole story. An old woman turning up from nowhere. Police, or government agents, or whatever hunting for her. It sounded pretty wild to him. Maybe these two were on something that gave them hallucinations.

'If she's got mates then why would she be wandering the streets?' he asked.

Both Kari and Jake shrugged. 'We don't know.'

'If we find them, at least we can tell them what's happened to her,' Kari said. She glanced helplessly at Jake then back at Razz. 'We just felt we *had* to do something.'

Razz shook his head doubtfully. This was all new to him. People risking their lives for someone they hardly knew.

'You'd be looking for a needle in an 'aystack,' he said.

'No.' Kari bent forward and took a piece of paper from one of the pockets of her bag.

'Do you know anything about the World-web?' Jake asked.

''Course,' Razz said indignantly. For the first time in his life he *didn't* want people to think he was stupid. 'The Baron's on it,' he said. 'And there's one or two places who let you get access, if you've got dosh, of course.'

'Of course,' Jake said.

'Who's the Baron?' Kari looked puzzled.

'He rules the roost around 'ere.'

'Oh,' Kari said. She glanced over her shoulder as if He might be standing behind her.

Jake took the bit of paper from her fingers and spread it out on the table.

'Look,' he said to Razz. 'This website address. We found it after Rachel got taken away. We tried to send a message but couldn't get it to go through. We worked out it's docklands, that's why we came here. We tried to find out what corporation it is but there weren't any files of that name. Does it mean anything to you at all?'

Razz stared at it.

Ra@starhost.dck/City.uk.

Blood pounded in his ears. His mind spun. It was the same as the one Jon had given him. The one he could use if he could get access to a mail facility. The one Jon had asked him not to show to anyone else.

His face stayed impassive as he tried not to give anything away. He was on to a really good thing here. These kids. They were from the country, they were obviously loaded, they were desperate to find these people. He didn't really understand why and he didn't really care.

All he knew was that if he played his cards right he could make a real killing here.

''ow much?' he hissed. He glanced round to check no one was listening.

Kari and Jake looked puzzled.

'How much, what?' Jake said.

''ow much will you give me if I help you?' Razz said.

Kari was staring at him. She shrugged. 'I don't know.' She glanced at Jake. 'Jake?'

Jake shrugged. 'Hundred?'

Razz swallowed and tried not to let them see his excitement. With a hundred Euros *and* the money he'd got for the software he could even afford to buy a few lotto tickets. If he won then maybe that dream of a shiny *new* drumset wasn't totally beyond reach after all.

'Er . . . one fifty,' he said.

Kari shook her head. 'I don't know if we could get that much.'

Razz shrugged. 'Too bad.'

Kari looked at Jake. 'OK,' she said. 'We'll get it somehow.'

Razz knew he should feel jubilant but for some reason he felt nothing at all.

He swigged the last of his tea and wiped his mouth on the back of his hand. 'Meet me 'ere tomorrow at ten and I'll see what I can do. You'd better have 'alf the money.'

'We told you,' Jake said. 'It all got pinched. You'll have to trust us.'

Trust? Razz looked at Jake, then at Kari. She was gazing at him beseechingly. Stupidly, crazily, he said, 'OK, then.' He stood up. 'See yer tomorrow.' He glanced outside. Pitch dark and raining. He'd have to find somewhere pretty quick if he didn't want to spend the night out in the open.

Kari reached out and tugged at his sleeve. 'Can't you take us now?'

'You must be joking,' he said. 'We'd never make it.'

'Do you know anywhere we could stay the night, then?'

He gazed at her, then at Jake. Then he shrugged. He'd got a place in mind. An old City bus that had been hijacked round one of the backstreets years ago. It was rusty and falling to bits but at least the roof was intact and they would be dry.

'Come with me if you want,' he said.

When Jake spotted it he gave a low whistle. 'Wow! Cool! Combustion engine. What happened to it?'

Razz shrugged. 'Got hijacked by terrorists.'

'Oh,' Jake said. 'Pity.'

Kari was walking beside Razz, carrying his board for him. She giggled as Jake hurried on ahead. 'Ignore him, he's crazy about old vehicles. Anything with an engine and he goes mad.'

Razz raised his eyebrows. He had heard that country people were nuts. It was obviously true.

The inside of the vehicle was still warm from the day's heat. Luckily, it was empty so they could spread themselves around.

Razz lay with his knees drawn up. He wasn't very comfortable but he'd slept in worse places. He could hear Kari and Jake murmuring to one another. He strained his ears but couldn't make out what they were saying. He wondered if they were girlfriend and boyfriend. They seemed pretty close—not lovey-dovey but really good friends. He felt a sudden, unexpected stab of envy. There wasn't anyone around this neck of the woods remotely like Kari. He only wished there was. The girls he knew had dirty rat-tailed hair and wore micro-skirts and white, pointy-heeled shoes that had been worn by a dozen other girls before them. Groups of them assembled on street corners cat-calling or giggling when he scooted past.

Then there was the woman Kari and Jake had told him about. Rachel. She must be a really good friend for them to risk everything coming here. He felt a stab of guilt. Maybe he shouldn't ask for their money. Maybe he should just take them to the Pool and not expect any Euros for the privilege.

Razz shifted, trying to get more comfortable. He

could hardly understand all the crazy thoughts going round in his head. He couldn't sleep either.

Sighing, he got up and lugged his radio down from the overhead rack. Outside, the rain had cleared away and the moon was shining. Two Drifters had set up home in a doorway opposite. Razz could just make them out in the white light. They were making themselves comfortable, spreading out blankets, covering themselves with polybags.

He switched his radio on, fiddled around trying to tune in to one of the pirate stations. He located one he liked, the one that played non-stop rock all night. He turned it up just loud enough to appreciate the heavy beat without telling the whole World they were there.

'Is that your kind of stuff?' Kari was kneeling in the seat in front and staring at him from over the back.

'Yeah.' He tapped his fingernails on the hard plastic of the radio case.

'Do you play?' she asked.

He turned his head, gazing up at her. 'Play?'

'An instrument.'

'Drums,' he said. 'But they got nicked.'

She spread her upper arms along the back of the seat and leant her chin on her clasped hands. 'I'm sorry,' she said. 'Will you get some more?'

'One day maybe.'

Kari was grinning. 'We could be a duo.'

'What kind of a duo?' He sat up, pushing his back against the side of the bus.

'A drum and flute duo.' She laughed this time. He could imagine her eyes lighting up. 'Be different, wouldn't it?'

'Is that what you play . . . flute?'

'Yep.'

Razz indicated his head towards Jake, dozing in spite of the noise. 'What's he play?'

She laughed again. 'Computer games.'

He stared at her then laughed too. Out loud, suddenly realizing it was the first time he'd done that for as long as he could remember.

8

The sun was coming up in overture of orange and black as they headed towards the river the following morning.

The pavements sparkled. The sky threw a fiery holocaust into pools of water left by the overnight rain. It was already warm. A mist was rising like phantasms from the river. Towards the estuary, a flock of gulls trailed behind the rubbish barges as they carved their way out to sea. Their cries and screams echoed eerily back towards Razz as he dragged his cart up and over the wall then waited for the others to catch up.

'Come on, you lot,' he called. He wanted to get to the Pool before there were too many people about. It was Saturday, the day of the big market when people flocked from all corners to get their goods for the week. He'd also got to find a new place to live. He couldn't spend forever dragging his stuff around.

Kari caught him up and stood a moment, staring at the rainbow of graffiti etched on the dilapidated hoarding that bordered one of the bomb sites.

'Are you coming or not?' Razz asked impatiently.

She turned. 'Oh, yes, sorry.'

Jake was staring at a foreign language motto carved over one of the doorways in the buildings along the bankside. 'Hey, this is cool,' he called. 'Anyone know what it says?' When they both shook their heads he pulled a notebook from his pocket and copied it down. 'I'll look it up when we get back,' he said, jogging over to them.

'You won't get back at this rate,' Razz grumbled.

'And if you don't get a bleedin' move on you won't get there in the first place.'

They hurried along beside him, skirting the fallen masonry, heading across the road and over the first barricade.

'Where exactly are we going?' Jake asked.

'I'll tell you when we get there,' Razz said.

'You don't have to be so grumpy,' Kari said. 'We *are* paying you after all.'

'Yeah,' he mumbled. 'Sorry.'

By the time they got there he'd told them his life story. He hadn't wanted to. Kari had dragged it out of him. She had a way of doing that. Making you say things you didn't mean to. Not that there was much to tell, really. It felt strange, talking to people who only knew about City life from their computer screens and TV sets.

'I always wanted to come,' Kari confessed.

'What, 'ere?' Razz couldn't believe she was telling the truth.

She gave a little laugh. 'Well . . . no . . . not here exactly.'

When they reached the entrance to the alleyway that led to the square they halted.

'Hang about,' Razz said. 'I'll see if it's safe.'

He looked around, frowning. For ages he'd had an odd feeling they were being followed. He hadn't told the others. Kari had been chatting away merrily, dragging out of him answers to her questions. She hadn't even seemed to notice when he kept glancing round. She probably thought he was keeping an eye on Jake. Jake had kept wandering off to look at things. To examine bits of old engines lying around, pick up bits of machinery or scraps of paper, old magazines that were littering the pavements. Once he'd climbed up on to the remains of the flyover and pointed to the entrance to the abandoned river tunnel.

'Where's that go?' he shouted.

'Nowhere,' Razz had shouted back. 'And if you don't get down we won't be going nowhere neither.'

He'd been lucky yesterday, not coming across anyone. In fact yesterday had been lucky altogether apart from his place getting turned over.

Razz dived along the alleyway, keeping low, kicking over the remains of the camp he'd destroyed the day before. He kept close to the wall, edging towards the end. He stopped on the corner, peering round to see if the coast was clear.

It was.

He motioned the others to follow. Kari was dragging his cart.

'Thanks.' He took the handle from her. His fingers brushed hers and he felt a bolt of something like electricity shoot up his arm. She grinned up at him.

'Good cart that,' she said.

He grinned back, swallowing, not really knowing what to say.

Jake was looking all around. The sun touched the jagged windows turning the glass fragments to a million sparkling diamonds. The glare made him screw up his eyes in a squint.

Eventually he swung round and looked at Razz. He frowned suspiciously. 'This can't be it.'

Razz dragged his eyes from Kari's. 'Yeah, it is,' he said. 'It's it.'

'Where are they, then?' Kari was beginning to look uncertain as well. She began to pace around, looking up, narrowing her eyes against the bright light.

Then she whirled on him. 'No one lives here, Razz. What are you playing at?' She ran across and tried to peer inside one of the broken windows, jumping up, not being able to see.

'It's deserted,' she shouted. She ran to the other side and did the same thing. Razz wanted to shout at her, tell her to stop, that everything was going to be all right if she just stood still and waited.

She ran back across and jumped on to the fountain wall to try to get a better view. She raised her arm . . .

Then, suddenly, there was a sound and a figure appeared in the doorway. Jon.

Razz blinked. Not only Jon but Others too. A stream of people coming out, heading their way through the dazzle of sunlight. He recognized one or two faces he'd seen the day before. They were hurrying, running towards them chattering in their own language. He felt a quick wave of panic as they bore down on them. Turn . . . run . . . It was all he could do to stay put.

Jon reached them first. He didn't even seem to see Razz, or Jake. He went right past. Kari was still poised on the wall of the fountain. He went and stood in front of her, staring at her with a kind of rapt expression on his face.

Kari swallowed and stared back. Her arm was still in mid air. It stayed there as if she'd been turned to stone.

Jon went on staring at her.

'Kari?' he said.

Then everyone crowded round and she disappeared from sight.

'It must have been Rachel,' Kari whispered as the people from *Starhost* ushered them inside.

Razz was still scared. He hated crowds. You never knew who might stick a knife in your back.

'What do you mean?' Jake hissed.

They were being taken up the stairs. The people were still talking among themselves. In the square, when Jon had turned and said, '*It's her, it's definitely her*', they had come to touch Kari's face, her hair, her hands before she even had time to speak. Razz had been scared they were hurting her. He hadn't known what to do, only elbow them aside and tell them to give Kari some air. Even then they went on touching her hair, her face as if they'd never stop.

'She must have mailed them and told them we might be coming,' Kari answered. 'I told you she left the bracelet on purpose,' she hissed in his ear. 'She *meant* us to find them.'

Razz heard. He still felt bewildered. 'What bracelet?'

Kari held up her arm and pointed to the one wedged between the circlets on her wrist. 'This one. It's Rachel's. It's got the website address on it.'

'Oh.' Razz wondered why she hadn't shown it to him before.

'Do you reckon she's got access to a machine, then— wherever they've taken her?' Jake asked, still puzzled.

Kari shrugged. 'Who knows.' Then her face lit up. 'I bet she used mine.'

'What do you mean?'

Razz was looking from one to the other.

Kari explained about Rachel going back upstairs the night they were running from Zeon. 'I bet she did it then,' she said. 'How else would they have known who I was?'

They were at the top now and heading towards the door. Kari stopped and caught her breath. Jake did too, staring up at the peculiar symbols with a frown on his face. Then he turned to Kari.

'They're the patterns you painted on your ceiling.'

She was breathing hard and staring at them with a dazed expression on her face. 'I know,' she said. 'That's really weird.'

Jon was behind them. 'You were talking about Rachel,' he said. 'When is she coming?'

Kari and Jake turned to face him. 'She's not,' Kari told him. 'That's why we're here.'

'Not coming?' Jon frowned. 'Why not?'

They had been taken to one of the rooms with comfortable, overstuffed chairs and gentle violin music playing in the background. Razz found himself liking it more and more. It made him relax, gave him the kind of feeling of well-being he wasn't at all used to.

As soon as they got in there Kari had started asking questions but Jon had held up his hand.

'You must tell me about Rachel first,' he insisted. 'It's vital we know.'

A young man in jeans and a white T-shirt had brought them a tray of drinks and sandwiches. He looked so much like Jon, Razz thought he must be his brother. Razz had wolfed the sandwiches down as if he hadn't eaten for a week. The others, too busy telling Jon what had happened, hardly touched theirs so Razz ate those as well.

When they finished their story Jon asked them lots of questions. Was Rachel all right? What had she told them? Did she leave anything behind?

Kari showed him the bracelet.

Jon held out his hand. 'Can I have it please, Kari?'

But Kari had put her arm behind her back. 'No,' she said. 'Rachel left it for me. Anyway, I want you to explain some things to *us* first.'

Razz had grinned to himself. Kari was learning fast.

Jon was pacing the room, biting his lip. 'I'm sorry, Kari,' he said. 'It'll have to wait.' Then he left for a while, telling them he would be back as soon as he could.

When he had gone they all began talking at once.

'The funny thing is,' Kari said, 'I know I've seen him somewhere before. And some of the other people. That girl with black hair . . . and that other fair-haired man in the blue sportshirt.' She shook her head. 'I wish I could remember where.'

'Think, Kari!' Jake urged.

'I am,' she said irritably. 'I've been thinking all the time. I just can't remember.'

'Anyway,' Razz said before an argument could break out. 'They're her friends all right, aren't they? I done what I said, didn't I?'

'Yes.' Kari turned towards him. Her face softened. 'Thanks, Razz. We would never have done it without you. As soon as we get back I'll send you the money, honestly.'

Razz felt his cheeks go red. Then, stupidly, he found himself saying something he never thought he'd hear himself say. 'It's OK,' he said. 'It don't matter.'

' 'Course it does,' Kari said.

But Razz shook his head. 'No. It don't, honestly.'

She was just about to argue some more when Jon came back into the room. 'We've got a good idea where they might have taken her.'

'Where?' Jake asked.

'A place called Blenham.'

'Blenham?' Kari looked thoughtful. 'I've heard of that. Wasn't it a palace or something?'

'A palace?' Razz said. 'Blimey. She ain't one of the royals, is she?'

Jon ignored his question. 'We've got contacts in other parts of the City. They just told us it was possible Rachel had been taken there.'

Jake was looking thoughtful. 'My mum was talking about Blenham once. Something about getting a job there.'

They all stared at him.

'A nurse in a palace?' Kari said. 'Sounds weird to me.'

Jake was still frowning. 'But if it's an old people's home,' he said, '*then* they might need nurses. Maybe it was a palace that they've turned into an old people's home. I've heard Mum say there's never enough places for them all.'

Kari was looking upset. 'I knew that's what they were going to do with her,' she said. 'She'll hate it, I know she will.'

'But why all those police?' Jake began.

Jon was shaking his head. 'No,' he said. 'It's not an old people's home. They think it's a government laboratory of some kind.'

'You're joking!' Kari looked at him in horror. 'What kind of laboratory?'

Jon shrugged. 'I'm not sure.'

Kari shook her head. 'Palaces, police . . . and now *government* laboratories. I *wish* someone would tell me what's going on.'

'Can't you find details on the web?' Jake asked before Jon could answer Kari's question.

Jon shook his head. 'It's restricted information. It'll need a real hacker to crack the password.'

Kari looked at Jake then back at Jon. 'Jake's brilliant at that,' she said.

'Well, not exactly brilliant,' Jake said with a shy grin. 'But I could have a go.'

'How long would it take?' Jon said.

Jake shrugged. 'Minutes . . . hours . . . days.'

'Why is it restricted?' Kari asked.

Jon bit his lip. 'I don't know,' he said although Razz didn't believe him. He could always tell when people were fibbing. Jon was hiding something and he wished he knew what it was.

Kari had obviously sensed it too. 'You know something else, don't you?' she said to Jon. 'I wish you'd tell us.'

'Look Kari,' Jon said. 'We *will* tell you everything but first we've got to concentrate on finding Rachel. She's in real danger.' He began pacing the room. He stared out of the window for a moment then turned to Jake. 'Will you have a go at locating that site?'

'Sure,' Jake said.

'Right.' Jon took him outside and was back within minutes.

'Razz, would you help us too?'

'Yeah,' Razz said. 'What do you want me to do?'

'Ask around, maybe *someone* will know what type of place Blenham really is and if it's possible to get in.'

Razz shrugged. 'Sure, no problem.'

His brain was in turmoil. Swampy. He knew more

than anyone else he'd ever met. He had told him he had worked for the government once, before he got chucked into prison for a while. If he didn't know something then no one would.

'Great,' Jon said. 'Will you do that now? Do you want to use another machine?'

'Machine?' Razz frowned. Then he grinned and tapped his temple. 'This is all the machine I need. And me skateboard.' He jumped up. 'I'll be there and back before you can say Jack Robinson.' His brain was whirling again. If he could find out before Jake hacked into those secret files then Kari might think he was brilliant too.

'Jack Robinson?' Razz realized Jon was speaking to him. 'Is that the person who might know?'

'Er . . . no,' he said. He headed towards the door.

Kari jumped up and ran after him. She put her hands on his arms.

'Be careful, Razz,' she said. 'And I'm sorry you've got dragged into this.'

'It's OK.' He gazed at her anxious face. She put her arms round him and gave him a brief hug. He put out a hand and touched her hair. It was soft and flowed through his fingers like warm honey. It didn't surprise him a bit. She smiled and let him go.

Jon had gone to look out of the window again. Suddenly he turned. 'You'll have to be careful, Razz, there's two men out there.'

Razz went to look. He recognized them at once. The two Drifters who had camped by the bus. It couldn't be a coincidence they'd turned up here. They would never have come all this way out unless they had a purpose. And now, seeing them in daylight, they weren't vagrants at all. They were wearing ragged clothes but their hair was neatly cut and they didn't have beards. And one was talking into a mobile. No wonder he'd had the feeling they were being followed. He could have kicked himself.

Kari was beside him, drawing in her breath sharply.

'They're Zeon's men,' she said. 'They must have followed us here.' She banged her fist on the window-sill. 'How could we have been so stupid!'

'Who's Zeon?' Jon asked.

Kari explained breathlessly, her words tumbling over one another in their rush to get out.

Jon was looking out of the window again. 'There's been people like them watching us before.'

'What for?' Razz asked. In his experience people who got spied on generally had something to hide.

But Jon ignored his question. Instead he said to Kari, 'If they've made Rachel tell them anything they could well be after you, Kari.'

Kari gulped. 'Me? What am I supposed to have done? If someone doesn't tell me what's going on soon I'll go ballistic!'

But all Jon did was turn to Razz. Razz decided he was better than any politician at evading questions.

'There's a back way . . . do you think you could get out without them seeing?'

Razz snorted. ''Course I can. Piece of cake.'

They left Kari and went to the end of a corridor that led to the fire escape. Jon keyed in a code and the door opened. A narrow, metal staircase spiralled down the outside wall.

'Will you be OK?' Jon said.

'No problem,' Razz assured him. He sounded a lot braver than he felt. Those guys didn't look a bit like policemen. You could always tell by the arrogant air of latent brutality that most police carried with them. These were different . . . stressed and anxious, cunning too. But there was something else about them Razz couldn't quite put his finger on.

Jon put his hand in his pocket and drew something out. It was a bracelet, just like the one Kari wore.

'Have you still got that bit of paper I wrote our address on?'

He shook his head. 'No . . . sorry. I lost it.'

Jon handed him the bracelet. 'If you can get access to a machine, it's on here. And you'll need a password. Starlight City. Will you remember that?'

'Yes,' Razz said.

He hadn't forgotten the address either but he took the bracelet just the same. If he never saw any of them again it would be a souvenir of his adventure. It felt strange in his fingers. Warm from the heat of Jon's pocket and reflecting a dozen hues from the lamp over the door. He stared at it for a minute, fascinated as always by the gaudy reflection of light. Then he quickly clipped it round his wrist. 'Thanks.'

At the bottom of the stairs he listened. He could hear the distant whine of a jet landing at the City airport and the hoot of a barge making its way upstream, the engine struggling against the strong current. A breeze had sprung up, tossing the dead leaves and litter around in a mad whirling tango.

Somehow or other he'd got to get his skateboard. He had left it in his cart, wedged under an overhang of concrete by the broken door to the lift. It would take him hours to get back without it. He would just have to risk they wouldn't spot him.

He tiptoed round the back, peering round the corner when he reached the end. He could just see them. One, still talking into his mobile. The other, sitting on the fountain wall taking swigs from a can of something and gazing up at the building. They'd never spot *Starhost* just by looking. It was strange but you couldn't see anything from the outside. The building looked just as desolate as all the others. Razz had never been able to work out quite how they managed to disguise themselves. He'd meant to ask but had got caught up in the whirl of activity at Kari's arrival and had forgotten all about it. There was no way those guys were ever going to know it was there unless Jon came out to meet them. And he wasn't likely to do that, was he?

Razz located his cart. He pulled out his board, tucked it under his arm and ran back the way he had come. He didn't stop running until he reached the river wall. He halted to get his breath, to listen if he was being followed. All he could hear was the sound of the water lapping the wall, the far distant hum of City traffic stuck on the bridge upstream, and the hammer-sound of a helicopter clamouring overhead. He squinted up into the sky but couldn't spot it anywhere.

He jogged along to the river path then got on his board, scooting the first hundred metres or so until there was a good clear run in front. The sun was low in the sky. If he was lucky he'd get back before dark.

'What's up, Razzle-Dazzle?' Swampy asked when he finally ground to a halt beside the stall. 'You never come back for them oranges. What happened?'

'Sorry.' Razz suddenly realized he was starving in spite of having eaten everyone's sandwiches. 'S'pose you've sold out today.'

'Yep, sold out and packed up. Come on, I'll buy you a cuppa.'

Razz put his hand on Swampy's arm. 'I want to pick your brains.'

'Right, do it over that tea.'

Ten minutes wouldn't hurt so he went with Swampy to the café. It was packed as usual, the air fuzzy with cigarette smoke and cooking fat.

'Heard you done a good deal yesterday,' Swampy said between gulps of hot tea.

'Yeah,' Razz said. He shifted his chair forward as two people barged through behind him.

'I heard your room got trashed.'

'Yeah.' There was no point in wondering how Swampy knew . . . everyone knew everything round here.

'Found anywhere else yet?'

'No.' Razz thought of his radio stowed away with his cart back at the Pool. He doubted he'd ever see either of them again. He looked across the table at Swampy. He was probably the oldest man he'd ever met. He'd got to be at least a hundred and twenty. Grizzled beard, eyes like bright beads embedded in his face, tanned skin carved into wrinkles by all weathers, old knitted woolly cap even in summer. All the wisdom of the World in his eyes.

'Swampy.' Razz leaned forward. 'You ever heard of a place called Blenham?'

'Blenham? 'Course I have,' Swampy laughed. 'It's northwest of 'ere. Once the palace of kings, now an old folk's dumping ground. People up Westend . . . that's the kind of place they put their granny in.'

Razz wished Swampy would keep his voice down. He didn't want *everyone* to know he was asking questions.

'Is that *really* what it is . . . an old folk's place?'

'Yeah, 'course.' Swampy drained his mug. He leaned forward. 'Why do you want to know? Going to book yourself in for your old age?' He chuckled and wiped tea from his beard with the back of his hand.

Razz laughed. 'No. I just 'eard someone talking about it and was curious, that's all. Do you know exactly where it is?'

'Upriver,' Swampy said unhelpfully. 'Miles up.'

'Oh.' Razz's mind was in a turmoil. So Blenham *was* an old folk's place. Or was that just what you were *supposed* to think? 'Could you get there by river?' Razz asked.

'Oh yes, my man. The king's barges used to plough up and down loaded with servants and footmen. Take you about a day I reckon. That's if you've got one of them power boats. If not it could take you a week.' Swampy chuckled.

A vision of a golden barge loaded with folk in fine clothes was flitting across Razz's imagination.

'What's it like?' he asked.

'What, Blenham? Oh . . . big old fancy place. Gardens as big as an 'ousing estate.' Swampy got up, still chuckling. 'Let us know if you manage to get a room booked.' He drained the last of his mug of tea and headed for the door.

Razz stood up too. 'Yeah . . . right. See you, Swampy. Ta for the tea.'

Razz finished his drink and left the café.

Outside, a chilly wind had sprung up. Razz tucked his board under his arm and turned up his collar. Swampy was across the road, talking to a couple of women camping in a doorway. Then he made off in the direction of the marshes where he lived.

Upriver, Razz thought. If they could get hold of a boat . . . Safer than going on foot. If they could avoid the patrols, that was. But where could they get one? Then his heart gave a quick thud. The old cruiser he'd seen moored at the foot of the river Stairs. If they could get the engine going they could use that. His heart gave another quick, wild beat of excitement. Then he sighed. It didn't look as if it had been used for years and they'd probably never get it started anyway.

But at least he'd found out about Blenham. Good old Swampy. When he'd found somewhere to kip for the night he'd be off back to the Pool first thing to tell them the good news. Razz fingered the bracelet, tucked under the cuff of his sweatshirt. He'd never get access to anyone's machine this late . . . if ever. Then he'd have to ask them how to work it and they'd want to know what the message was about. It would be much better to go and tell them himself. See Kari's reaction to the good news.

Behind him, the café door opened. He was just about to move out of the way when he felt a hand on his arm.

'Just a minute, son. We want a word with you.'

Razz turned and stared into the dark brown, anxious eyes of Zeon.

PART THREE

At Blenham

9

I was still waiting for Jon to tell me what was going on an hour later. He'd gone off with Razz to show him the back way out and that's the last I'd seen of him.

I wandered down the corridor and into a room where people were working on their computers. A dark-haired girl turned in her chair. Before her screensaver butted in I could see she was working on some kind of musical score.

I stared at her. Again I had a really weird feeling. I *knew* I'd seen her somewhere before.

I was just about to ask her where it was likely to have been when she logged off and stood up.

'Has Jon taken you round?'

I shook my head. 'No.'

'Come on, I'll take you on a tour.'

'My name's Eliz,' she told me as she led me back down the corridor.

'I'm Kari,' I told her.

'I know,' she said gravely.

'It's funny,' I said. 'But I'm sure I've met you before.' I was still racking my brains.

But instead of suggesting anything she just looked cagey and said, 'Hasn't Jon told you *anything*?'

I shook my head.

'He will, honestly.'

'Can't *you* tell me?' I asked.

'No. Sorry. It's up to Jon, I'm afraid.'

'Is he your boss, then?'

'Kind of,' she said.

By now we'd reached the room at the end of the corridor. She pushed the door open. 'This will interest you,' she said.

But before we could go in, there was a shout from along the corridor. Jake. I left Eliz and ran along to see what was up.

When I got there he was whooping and spinning around in his chair like a maniac.

'I've got it!'

He leapt up and grabbed hold of me and whirled me round. Eliz arrived and grinned broadly when she saw Jake acting like a crazy person.

Jake sat back down in front of the screen, keyed something in and up it came . . . Blenham.

Jon appeared. He looked tired and bleary eyed as if he hadn't slept for a week. It had been really weird. When I first saw him it was all I could do to stop myself hugging him. It was just that it was strangely like seeing an old friend. We had stared at each other for a few seconds. I could see his aura . . . pale gold and yellow. And when he smiled so softly at me I had suddenly and for no apparent reason wanted to cry.

But now his aura was dull and sad. It brightened a bit when Jake pointed excitedly to the screen.

'Look!'

In front of us was a huge old house . . . a palace. Its massive front door was flanked by stone columns. Its rooftops were like a city of chimneys and statues. The front was covered with elegant, arched windows. There was a long drive flanked by vast green lawns with more statues and lakes and trees. The name underneath . . .

Blenham.

Everyone was leaning forward, staring at it as if it was something from another planet.

'That's it,' Jake said. He sat back, looking smug. Jon was standing at his shoulder. Jake turned to speak to him. 'I'll have a go at hacking into their files.'

Jon patted his shoulder. 'Thanks,' he said. He peered

closer, narrowing his eyes as if he was trying to see right inside the screen.

Jake was tapping away on the keyboard. I guessed he was trying to access Tourguide, an interactive journey round the house.

Half an hour later he was still trying.

'We should get going.' I was feeling really anxious by now. 'The sooner we get Rachel out, the better. Jon, you come too. They'll take more notice of you.'

I knew we had to get a move on. While we were all here discussing things, poor Rachel was locked away in this vast, gloomy place that looked like a prison to me. I had remembered reading it was once the palace of kings and queens and could just imagine them riding up and down the long drive in their limousines and playing old-fashioned games on the lawns in summer. But I'd got a terrible feeling no one did anything like that at Blenham any more.

Jon was biting his lip. 'It won't be that easy,' he said.

'Why not?' I demanded to know.

All Jake had managed to do was access a mapsite. He printed it out. Blenham was close to the river. The same river that snaked its way through the City, through the docklands then north west through kilometres of suburban housing, factories and estates, meandering through another city until it turned into a little stream then disappeared altogether. The roads would be impossible but there was bound to be a tramline that went that way.

'I . . . we . . .' Jon looked helplessly at the others. 'We don't have any ID,' he said eventually. 'We'd never get through the turnpikes.'

'But *we* can,' I said. 'Can't we, Jake?' Luckily, ours had been in our inside pockets when we got mugged.

'No problem,' Jake said although I could tell by his voice that he thought it might be a problem.

It didn't occur to me at the time that what Jon had said was really weird. Everyone had ID. You couldn't move without it. You couldn't catch a tram, get in a mall, a moviedrome, go to Westend, or Eastend, or anywhere. That's why there were so many ghettos, people living in areas they couldn't move out of. No one lived in a place like this by choice, surely? And then later, when I *did* think about it—it all seemed to fit. That was why *Starhost* was stuck out here. The people who ran it must be illegal immigrants. How they got to be friends with Rachel I had no idea. Perhaps she was one too and *that's* why the police were after her.

For some reason Razz hurtled into my thoughts. My heart did a little skip. I could still see his hazel-coloured eyes gazing at me. I wondered where he was and if he was thinking about me. He'd been gone for hours and we hadn't heard a thing.

Jon was shaking his head. 'No, it's too dangerous. Anyway, Kari, we want you to stay here.'

'I want to stay here too,' I said. 'But that's not what we came here for. We came to help Rachel.'

I felt I was being torn into two pieces. Half of me wanted to stay with Jon and the Others, the other half had to find Rachel. I couldn't explain to anyone why I felt like that.

I told Jon.

'We've got to go,' I said. 'I'm sorry.'

Jon's eyes grew sad with resignation.

'All right, Kari,' he said with a sigh. He put his hands on my arms. 'Please be careful.'

' 'Course we will,' I said.

Later, Jake said to me, 'I reckon we'd better e-mail the parents. Say we're getting on great at Vinny's, otherwise they're going to start asking questions. I'll do it now so they can access it in the morning.'

He fixed it so there would be no sender's website address on the message.

After that he spent half the night trying to get more information about Blenham from the web. He finally discovered that all Blenham's treasures had been sold to foreign investors and the house had been closed up after the downfall of the royals. Then it had been turned into an old folk's home. So Jon's friends were wrong. Blenham *wasn't* a government laboratory at all. It was bad enough though. I couldn't stand to think of Rachel shut up in there. She would hate it. Sitting in rows and rows staring at the TV. She'd never get a chance to gaze at the stars or play the piano or take one of those country walks she told me she loved. We had to get her out.

'But if that's what it really is,' Jake was saying with his usual aggravating logic, 'why isn't there any info on the web? You'd have thought they would want people to know it's there. Look,' he pointed to the screen. '2001— Blenham became Happy Days Retirement Home. Then zippo . . . nothing.'

'There's only one way to find out,' I said.

Jake grinned up at me. 'Right,' he said. 'Let's make plans.'

Later, I managed to doze on one of the sofas in the reception room. I lay for a while listening to the far off sounds of the city, the singing of the wind around the rooftops. I heard the sound of the heli-patrols drumming their way to and fro across the Cityscape. One came right overhead and I could see the laser-lights, flashing red, then green, throwing rainbow shadows through the windows. Then it gunned away, satisfied there was nothing to investigate.

I'd tried to find Jon again. I'd wandered up and down the corridors like an inquisitive ghost. Peeping in one room after another. Everywhere was deserted. All the rooms in darkness, all the machines in stand-by. I went down to the ground floor with the intention of looking in the basement. But the door was stuck and wouldn't budge. So I went back up again. I couldn't work out where everyone had gone. Eventually I gave up.

It was about midnight when I woke from a restless doze and went to see how Jake was doing. Outside, the night was a vault of a million stars. I stood a minute to

105

gaze out of the window. The City sparkled all around me, an endless expanse of blazing lights to the horizon. Vehicle headlights, a huge motionless necklace of pearls, were strung along the flyovers as far as you could see. Then one would break away as it got through the turnpike and headed for the City centre. It was a totally alien, scary kaleidoscope World. I suddenly felt a sharp pang of homesickness. Damien, safely asleep in his bed. Mum, probably asleep too. Dad, hunched in front of his screens whatever time of night or day it was. The smells of the countryside seeping through the shutters on still, warm summer evenings.

When I went back to Jake he looked shattered. His eyes were red with fatigue and his shoulders drooped. I put my hand on his arm.

'Leave it for now,' I said. 'I've been looking for Jon. I want him to explain things to us before we leave.'

Jake swung round to face me. 'Have you noticed how he changes the subject every time we ask him?'

'Yes, that's why I want to pin him down.'

'Can't you find him then?'

I shook my head.

But Jake knew somewhere I hadn't been.

'The penthouse,' he said. 'I heard someone say they were going up there.'

I hadn't even realized there was one.

Jake took me to a flight of stairs that I'd thought led up to the rooftop.

Half-way up I suddenly stopped and caught my breath. I put my hand on Jake's sleeve. 'Hang on . . . listen.'

A whole symphony of sound came rolling down towards us. Soft at first, then getting louder and louder as the music reached a crescendo. It sounded as if there was a whole orchestra playing up there. I recognized the piece. The Millennium concerto it was called. Strings whirling and dancing, trumpets shouting, drums banging like firecrackers exploding in the sky. The score was written fifty years ago in celebration of the new millennium.

I stood there, frowning. My ear had caught a gap. One of the flutes was missing.

My heart skipped a beat. Just at that moment I would have given anything in the universe to fill that space.

The sound echoed and bounced and thumped down the staircase to surround us. I could see Jake was as starstruck as me even though he was usually only into the heavy rock stuff. When it finished, the silence was deafening. Then we heard a smattering of applause, the tapping of violin bows and the players chattering to one another excitedly.

'Wow!' Jake breathed. 'Someone's got a brilliant sound system.'

But I knew it wasn't that.

'Come on, let's have a look.'

I pushed open the double doors, just a crack at first and peeped through. Jake must have heard my sharp intake of breath because he nudged me. 'What's going on?'

I stood back so he could see them. There must have been a hundred musicians sitting round the edge of a huge, circular penthouse room. They were all the people we'd seen working the machines. Jon was there too, standing on a box in the centre with a baton in his hand.

'Wow!' Jake turned to me, his eyes wide with disbelief. Then they got bigger as some of the guitarists and drummers started playing again. This time it was a wild rock number that brought a broad grin to Jake's face.

'Wow!' he breathed again as if it was the only word he knew.

I couldn't say anything. There seemed to be a huge lump of something stuck in my throat. To play with a real live orchestra. It was something I'd dreamed of ever since I was a little kid. A thought flitted into my head. If they were a flute short then maybe . . .

Then we heard a voice behind us. Eliz. I didn't know how long she'd been there.

'Why don't you go in?'

'Will they mind?'

'Mind?' she said. 'They've been hoping you'd come.'

As soon as we got inside someone shoved a flute at me. It was the most beautiful one I'd ever seen. I ran my fingertips over it then looked at Jake. He grinned and nodded his head.

'Go on,' he said.

And when I looked there was an empty place in the woodwind section just as somehow I knew there would be.

A man with an oboe sat tapping his hands and feet and waving his head in time to the heavy drum beats and frenzied twanging guitars. He smiled at me as I edged along towards him. He patted the chair beside him as if he'd been expecting me all along.

I sat with the flute on my lap, waiting for the rock song to finish. When it finally did, everyone cheered and clapped. Jake was standing by the door waving his arms around applauding like crazy.

Then everything went quiet and Jon turned slowly to look at me. I felt his eyes burning into me. He held out his hand to me and I knew there was nothing in the universe that could have stopped me sliding my way in between the musicians and going to clasp hold of it. It was as if I was being drawn towards him on invisible threads.

'We hoped you'd hear us, Kari,' he said as I reached him.

Holding my hand, he turned and gazed at the grand piano standing silently in one corner of the room. 'We wish Rachel was here with us too,' he said.

And as I played the flute, the notes weaving and dancing up into the glass roof of the penthouse room, it suddenly came to me. How some of the pieces of the puzzle fitted neatly into one another.

Why I was here. Why they wanted Rachel.

Because . . . without us, the orchestra wasn't complete.

But that still left a lot of questions unanswered. Were these people really illegal immigrants? If so, where did they come from? And why didn't they try to get Eurocitizenship? Then they wouldn't have to hide out here disguised as the *Starhost* company when they should by rights be telling the whole World what great and wonderful musicians they were.

'But loads of people play the flute and piano,' Jake said to me the following day. 'Why does it have to be you and Rachel?'

'I don't know,' I said. 'When I asked Jon he just said it had to be us.'

We'd set off just as the sun was creeping up over the horizon. We made sure there was no sign of Zeon's men then everyone piled out of the building to see us go. They looked sad. Some of them were trying not to cry. I could tell how scared Jon was to let us go although he didn't say anything. As we headed for the alley and turned to give them all one last wave I felt my heart was breaking.

'We'll be back, don't worry.' Jake put his arm round me and hugged me to him. 'They're dying to see Rachel and you've got to hear that piece they promised to compose for you.'

I was too choked up to answer him. I knew it was silly. I'd only known them for a little while but it was like leaving friends I'd been close to all my life.

'We'll stick to the river,' Jake said. 'That way we shouldn't get lost. That's what Razz did on the way here.'

When Jake said Razz's name all my worries came crowding back. 'He can look after himself,' Jake had said when I told him. 'He's a street-kid, remember? He'll be fine.'

I tried to push my fear to the back of my mind. To the place where I store all the things I can't bear to think about. It didn't work. Razz kept crashing into my thoughts like a certain melody that you can't get off your brain. His name was whirling around in my head. Razz . . . Razz . . . it was almost as if he was doing it on purpose.

Jake was plodding along the river road with his head down. We passed one or two people: a man fishing in the murky water, a couple of girls with babies strapped to their backs sorting through a garbage heap. An old woman rummaging through stuff in a skip and muttering to herself. None of them took any notice of us. If we'd used our brains we'd have come dressed like this in the first place. No one looked at a ragged pair of urchins plodding along. We'd swapped our bright ruckbags for an old torn, brown one we'd found in a heap of rubbish in the alleyway near *Starhost*. We'd dumped it in Razz's cart and pulled that along behind us. Now, we just looked like anybody else.

'I still don't understand why Jon wouldn't explain things,' Jake was complaining.

'He promised he would,' I reminded him. 'When we come back with Rachel.'

'*If*, you mean.' Jake sounded unusually gloomy.

'He did say why it was best if we didn't know yet,' I reminded him. 'If we don't know anything then we can't tell anyone anything, can we?'

By now we'd reached the place where a steep flight of stone stairs led down to the river. The murky water was lapping round the hull of an old motor boat. The submarine yellow paint was cracked and peeling and the canvas canopy was tattered and torn. There was a name on the side, faded, but I could just make it out. *Jetstream*.

I stood for a minute staring at it. The seed of an idea was germinating in my brain. There wasn't any need for us to go back to the terminal. We'd probably never find it anyway. We could get to Blenham by water . . . *if* we had a boat.

'Come on, Kari,' Jake was calling impatiently. He had dragged the cart up and over a pile of rubble and was waiting for me to catch up.

'Come here,' I called. 'Come and look at this.'

He rocked and rolled the cart back over the debris and came to see what I was on about.

When he saw the boat he gave a low whistle. 'Wow! Four-berth cabin cruiser circa 1999 . . . inboard twelve cylinder engine. It doesn't look as if she's been cruising anywhere for years.'

'Let's look.' I ran down the stairs, grabbed one of the mooring ropes and hauled her close enough for me to jump on board.

'Hey, Kari, be careful.' There was panic in Jake's voice as he hopped down after me.

But I was already peering in under the canopy. The cockpit was full of rubbish but the steering wheel and instruments looked as if they were intact. I lifted the flap and clambered inside. Jake followed.

I turned to him. 'Could you get it going, do you think?'

He blinked. 'What this?'

'Yes, of course, *this*,' I said impatiently. 'If you could get it going we could go upriver . . . straight to Blenham. We wouldn't need to get a tram.'

Jake dragged his map from his pocket. He gazed at it for a minute. Then he looked at me. 'Yeah,' he said. 'You're right.' He put the map back and looked around.

'Hop up on the seat,' he said and when I did he bent down and lifted a hatch that had been under my feet. Inside was the engine. He knelt down and fiddled around for a while. Then he shook his head. 'I need a handbook.'

'I'll look.' I went down into the cabin. It was a mess. Broken bottles, a tatty old sleeping bag, a pile of used hypos. It stank too. Of river water and alcohol and other things I didn't like to think about. I opened the sink unit drawers and searched in the cupboards. Then, in a little cupboard under what looked like some kind of heater, I found it. The engine manual. I found something else too. A can half full of fuel.

Jake studied the book for a while then looked up. 'If all the bits are here I reckon I can do it,' he said. 'I'll need oil, though and some dry cloths.'

'I'll find them.' I jumped off and ran back up the stairs, grabbed the cart and dragged it along the wharfside. The two girls were still scrabbling about on the garbage heap. They didn't give me a second glance. I went to the skip and found some old clothes that would do as rags. After tossing aside cans and bottles and plastic sacks full of soggy things I located a box full of empty plastic oil containers. I shook one and something sloshed about in the bottom. I undid them all, tipping the few grammes of oil left in each into one carton. By the time I'd finished it was almost full. I loaded the things into the cart and ran back, out of breath, my heart pounding like mad.

Jake was flat on his stomach in the cockpit, his head buried in the engine.

Ages later, he said, 'OK, turn it on.'

He had already wangled a crooked bit of wire into the ignition and pulled out the choke.

The engine turned but wouldn't fire. Jake sat back on his haunches. I couldn't help laughing at him. His arms were black up to the elbows and he had a long smear of oil across his cheek. He leant down and fiddled again.

'Now try.'

We both cheered as the engine groaned and bubbled then suddenly gunned into life. I put my arms round him and gave him a great hug.

'Jake, you're magic.'

He grinned. 'Yeah, I know.'

I laughed. 'I knew all that studying you do would come in really useful one day.'

I clambered back on to the quayside and dragged Razz's cart on board. Then I untied the ropes and shoved off with a long pole I'd found on deck. Jake pulled back the throttle and we wobbled slowly out into the middle of the river. On the wharfside the two girls with babies stared at us curiously as we sailed away, round the corner and out of sight.

The only thing I felt bad about was leaving Razz behind.

10

No one took a blind bit of notice of our little boat, chugging its way upstream. Through the City centre with its massive white buildings and teeming traffic. Sailing under bridges where trams sung overhead and goods' trains roared their way towards the City railheads. Past the red-brick prison that had been a power station in the last century. No one seemed to think it odd or unusual, two people looking like ragamuffins in a battered old cruiser out for a day's ride.

Only it took much longer than that. First we ran out of fuel.

'What's wrong.' I looked at Jake in alarm as the engine suddenly spluttered and stopped and we found ourselves drifting helplessly backwards with the current.

'Fuel,' he said. 'Now what are we going to do?'

'Yell?' I suggested. There were plenty of boats about. Someone would help us, surely?

As it turned out, a river warden came to our rescue. She didn't bat an eyelid when we flashed our ID. She just towed us to the nearest marina where we filled our tank and the spare can, then went off mumbling something about kids being in charge of boats when they didn't know what they were doing.

Jake and I couldn't believe it.

'It's because we stayed cool,' he said with a grin.

'I didn't feel cool.' I'd had to sit down in the cockpit my legs were shaking so much.

'You on holiday?' asked the boy who filled us up. He eyed *Jetstream*, grinning. 'Bit of an old wreck, isn't she?'

'Cheek! Good old boat, this.' I'd recovered from our scare, taken off my jacket and was sitting on the top in my ratty old T-shirt enjoying the sun. I'd decided I liked wearing old clothes. You didn't have to worry if they got torn or dirty.

The boy grinned again as Jake handed over some of the Euros Jon had given us.

'See you on the way back,' the boy called.

The river police stopped us just as it was getting dark. Speeding towards us in their sleek patrol launch. They moored up alongside and one of them came on board.

'Remember—keep cool,' Jake warned. 'They're probably looking for drugs or guns.'

We had already decided what we would say if they stopped us. Since leaving the marina, we'd bluffed our way through locks where each guard insisted on seeing our documents. Sailed under more bridges, past vast estates of suburban housing, through a park with trees and greenhouses full of exotic plants, more and more houses and ramshackle factories and shopping malls. I began to think Blenham was on the other side of the World.

But the police didn't seem to be looking for drugs or anything. They just scanned our ID then asked us where we were heading. In spite of their friendly manner I felt really nervous. If they ran a check and contacted our parents then the next time we were stopped we could be carted off back home.

'To visit my auntie.' I was surprised how easy it was getting to tell fibs. 'She lives upriver . . . near Blenham. Any idea how long it'll take us?'

My heart thudded wildly as the policewoman took our cards out of her scanner and handed them back.

'A good while yet,' she said. She made a sweeping movement with her arm. 'This is all private along here, stockbrokerbelt. If you stop here you're likely to get arrested. And you can't travel after dark,' she added. 'So you'd better find somewhere to moor for the night as soon as you can. An official site, mind you, otherwise you'll get picked up for being Drifters.'

I swallowed. By the look of us, it was a wonder she hadn't thought we were Drifters anyway.

'Right,' I managed to say. 'We will. Thanks.'

She peered at the faded river licence stuck to the windscreen. 'That's out of date by the looks of it.'

Before I could think of an answer Jake poked his head out of the side of the canopy. 'We know.' He grinned cheerily up at her. 'The old tub hasn't been out for years. We've applied for a new one but it hasn't come through yet. Sorry.'

She took out her pocket PC and keyed something in. 'OK,' she said. 'Make sure you display it when it comes through.' She eyed the peeling hull. 'You sure this is seaworthy?'

'We're going to do it up when we get to my auntie's,' I said.

'About time by the looks of it.' She grinned at us. 'Have a good trip,' she added good-naturedly.

'Thanks.' I stood on the deck and waved as they left, the sharp bow of their launch slicing through the water like an arrow.

We'd been going for another half an hour when Jake called from the cockpit, 'Is that a mooring place over there?'

It was. Notices told us that we weren't allowed to stay more than twelve hours. That was plenty long enough.

There were a couple of cruisers moored up in the same place. Bright shiny ones, with sleek hulls and satellite masts and gaily coloured curtains at their windows. On the bank, a family were having a barbecue. They eyed *Jetstream* curiously and I heard someone pass a rude comment then everyone laughed.

'Ignore them,' Jake said. His eyes twinkled. 'They're just jealous.'

We slept like logs in spite of the family next door making a row until well after midnight.

116

When that finally quietened down, I lay in my bunk, curled up like a little kid. The night sounds of the river seemed to make me relax. You couldn't even hear the hum of traffic or the drone of jet engines. There was only a twitter now and then from a solitary river bird and the slap, slap of the water against the hull. It seemed like a melody, lulling us to sleep. Before I drifted off, Razz blundered into my thoughts. I wondered if he had got back to Jon only to find that we'd already gone. I wondered if I would ever see him again.

I was up as soon as it began to get light. I poked my head out of the canopy. The river was still and quiet in the dawn air. An eerie mist was rising from the water. A spiderweb, woven overnight between the mooring ropes, was hung with crystal. The mist covered the canopy, the decks of the neighbouring cruiser, with a soft cottonwool mantle of grey. A gentle breeze touched my face with dewy fingers. I took a deep breath and was just about to clamber outside when a great bird rose from the bank opposite and flew upriver, disappearing into the mist like the echo of a departing ghost. The sun was just rising, a globe of gold peering above the rooftops to welcome the day.

Jake's voice made me jump.

'Shall we get going? The sooner we get there, the better.'

I turned. 'Yeah, OK.'

'It must have been a grey-coat,' Jake said later when I told him about the bird. 'They're pretty rare.'

'I know,' I said. 'I'm not daft.'

'Sorry,' Jake said.

That's the trouble with brainy people, they think they're the only ones who know anything.

By the time the mist had cleared and the sun was blazing overhead, the novelty of cruising was wearing off. It seemed we had been going for ever. We had sailed past housing estates and factories, through another city where spires dreamed in the morning sun. Then, just as we felt ready to give up, the buildings flanking the river began to gradually thin out and we were cruising past green fields. And suddenly, there it was. Blenham. Standing like a huge stone celebration cake well within sight of the river.

Jake spotted it first.

I was at the steering wheel while he sat on the deck gazing ahead. He suddenly stood up making the boat rock violently. He pointed and yelled excitedly.

'Kari . . . there it is!'

I poked my head out. My pulse drummed with excitement. We'd done it . . . we'd really done it.

But Blenham wasn't a bit like we imagined. The house looked the same but all the rooftop statues were gone and a lot of the windows had been boarded up. The sweeping gardens were wild, overgrown, trees gone mad. Grass and weeds had choked the lakes to death.

Worst of all, there was a tall, electrified fence all around the house. My heart plummeted. Old people's home? A prison camp more like. Surveillance systems . . . closed-circuit cameras at intervals along the fence. Huge laser-lights to blaze into life if there was any movement after dark. It wasn't like any old people's home I'd ever read about.

I stood there, staring. A blue haze of misery settled all around me. There was no way we were going to be able to sneak in. Jon's friends were right. It *was* a government establishment. A laboratory. A prison. What could Rachel have done that made them bring her to a place like this?

Jake turned the wheel and drove the boat to the opposite bank. 'We'd better moor up here and decide what to do,' he said.

Five minutes later we were standing together on dry land staring at the house. Jake tipped his cap to the back of his head. 'Do you still want to try to get in?'

' 'Course I do.'

'How?' Jake said.

'No idea,' I answered forlornly.

In my dreams I'd imagined rescuing Rachel, taking her to the boat and sailing back downstream to live happily ever after. But all that was just pie in the sky. You'd need to be a magician to get in this place. Our long journey upriver had been for nothing.

I sat down and drew my knees up to my chin. Jake plonked himself down beside me.

'I know,' he said suddenly. 'Let's go back downstream. Leave the boat where it can't be seen then walk to the house.'

I stared at him. Had the sun driven him off his trolley?

'What?' I said. 'What good will that do?'

'We could just brazen it out,' he said. 'Say we've come to visit Rachel. Once we get inside . . . '

'They won't let us in,' I said scornfully. 'I've got a feeling that anyone kept in here won't be allowed visitors.'

Jake had picked a stalk of grass and was chewing it absent-mindedly. 'But don't you see, Kari,' he said, 'Jon thinks they could be looking for you anyway. If you just turn up then they're bound to let you in. Zeon knows who you are.'

I shook my head. 'I still can't understand why Jon thinks they'll be looking for me.' It had been bugging me ever since he said it.

Jake shrugged. 'Depending on what Rachel's told them,' he reminded me.

'Yeah, but what *could* she tell them?'

Jake shrugged again. 'That you and your family sheltered her, that you took her to the tunnel to escape from the police.'

I shook my head. 'No, I told you. He wasn't interested that we'd broken the law. He was only interested in Rachel.'

'And maybe you,' Jake said.

119

My brain went into overdrive. Jake was right. We didn't really have any option. The only way we were going to get in was through the front door. If Jon was right and Zeon was looking for me then he'd be glad I'd turned up. And once we were inside, all we had to worry about was getting out.

I jumped up. 'OK, come on then.'

We sailed back downriver and moored up under a willow tree. We pulled *Jetstream* as far out of sight as possible. The last thing we wanted was anyone stealing her. She was our route to freedom.

We made our way across a field, clambered over the gate and headed off down the road towards the big house.

We tramped up a long drive flanked on either side by weeds and a thick tangle of brambles.

'Something's coming,' Jake hissed and we dived for cover.

A van whirred past. It had *Next-day Linen Service* written on the side.

Suddenly, round a bend, the gate loomed up ahead. There were security guards, a barrier. We stopped for a minute, watching as the van driver flashed his pass and the bar went up to let him through.

Jake put his hand on my arm. 'Keep cool, OK.'

I was staring at a huge sign that straddled the footpathway.

HAPPY DAYS RETIREMENT HOME
MANAGER—MARION KAPOOR

As well as the guards, several uniformed men were strolling around or standing in little groups. They eyed us curiously as we sauntered towards them. They looked sociable enough but you would have to be blind not to notice the bulge underneath their jackets. Guns.

'I don't know if I can do this,' Jake murmured. I could see a little red cloud of fear hovering over his head. When I clutched his hand it was damp with sweat.

'Yes, you can,' I said. 'They can't *do* anything to us, can they?'

'You're joking,' Jake said. 'No one knows we're here, remember.'

'Yes, they do,' I argued. 'Jon and the others, they know.'

'But they can't do anything. No one knows they exist.'

I swallowed. Jake was right as usual. If we disappeared off the face of the World no one would ever find us. Vinny would say we hadn't been there at all, that we'd told her we were going to the City for a bit of fun. And you could vanish without trace in the City. Two country kids, run away from home. So, what's new? We might go on the web for a while, listed as missing persons, but only for a week or two. The lists were too long for anyone to stay on there for more than that. We would be just like those people I'd read about in Timescan—the ones who claimed they'd been abducted by aliens. Except *they* turned up again and it was just possible that we never would.

I was just about to say I was getting cold feet when we heard a car behind us. A limousine with blacked out windows purred past and drew up at the gate. Jake grabbed my arm and pulled me to one side. The window slid down, then the door opened and the driver got out, fumbling in his back pocket for his ID.

I drew in my breath.

Zeon.

Suddenly, one of the back doors burst open and a figure dived out. A tall, skinny figure in a ragged, steel-studded denim jacket and jeans, a red sparkler in one ear, and wild eyes that darted desperately to and fro as he made a mad dash for freedom.

I clutched Jake. 'It's Razz!'

Jake was holding me too. 'Stay cool, OK?'

But I *had* to do something. Zeon, the guards . . . they all shot after him, grabbing him before he could get more than a few metres. He was felled by a flying rugby tackle. I heard him shouting and swearing at them as he struggled to get up again. One was sitting on his back, the other had grabbed handfuls of his hair. Zeon bent down to get hold of his legs.

I shot forward, wrenching away from Jake. I hurtled towards them and seized hold of the man sitting on Razz's back. I yanked his head so hard he yelled in surprise and tumbled backwards on to the road. Razz struggled free and was up and away, running like the wind. He turned, once, to stare at me over his shoulder. Jake was dodging around, trying to bar the way as the guards dived after him.

But it was no good. People materialized out of thin air. They grabbed Jake and Razz, twisted their arms behind their backs and frog-marched them back to Zeon. Zeon had a face like thunder. He had straightened his jacket and brushed down his trousers, wrenched his mobile phone from his pocket, and was busy yelling something into it.

I got hauled to my feet and dragged across. Zeon switched off his phone and stuck it back in his pocket. He stared at me as if I was a vampire risen from the grave. The others brought the boys back, still struggling, to stand beside me.

Zeon barked a command.

'OK, let them go.'

He was staring at me. His quick, dark eyes were glowing with triumph. As if he'd had a scheme that had succeeded. And I knew with a sinking heart that he had. He knew we would come here to find Rachel. His air of anxiety had gone. Instead he looked smug. A broad grin spread slowly across his face. He had got exactly what he wanted.

Rachel and . . . me.

But why he wanted us, I still didn't know.

11

'You all right, Kari?' Razz looked at me anxiously.

We'd all been bundled into the back of the car and whisked through the barrier.

'Yes,' I said. 'Are you?' We were all squashed up together. I couldn't help thinking how good-looking he was. He'd obviously had the chance to wash his face and hair since we saw him last. His skin was a dark bronze and his curls shone with golden lights.

He managed a grin. 'Yeah.'

He didn't look all right. He had a mega bruise on his forehead where he'd hit the ground. It was already turning canary yellow. His jacket was torn, his hair was a great mass round his head where it had come out of its band. He shook it out of his eyes and gazed at me. 'I didn't think I'd ever see you again.'

'I didn't think I'd see you either.' I kept gazing back at him.

The car was swishing down the long drive that stretched like a grey ribbon between the gate and the huge sweep of stone steps that led up to the column-flanked front door of the house.

'Please . . . ' Jake rolled his eyes. He was slumped in the corner trying to hold together the two sides of his T-shirt where it had got ripped. 'Is that all you two can think about?'

Razz went cherry red. I couldn't help grinning.

'When did they pick you up?' Jake asked him.

He explained. 'And when I sussed out why they wanted me,' he said in a low voice, 'I got rid of the bracelet. There's no proof now I've ever been to *Starhost*. They can do what they like to me but I shan't tell 'em anything. I liked those people there and I'm not going to get them into trouble.'

I squeezed his hand. 'You're brilliant, Razz.'

He went ruby red this time. But I was right, he *was* brilliant. And if they found Jon and the others and deported them, we'd never forgive ourselves. We all knew what happened to people who'd had to escape from their own countries. Especially when they were forced to go back.

I shuddered, just thinking about it.

I was feeling for my own bracelet . . . cool, yet it seemed to be burning a hole in my wrist. I had to get rid of it. I unclasped it and shoved it down the back of the seat.

I looked out of the window, gazing upwards. There it was again. A big sign. HAPPY DAYS RETIREMENT HOME. Who were they kidding?

Two women in white lab coats stood on the threshold of the massive entrance, waiting like spiders ready to pounce on their prey.

As soon as the car drew up they hurried down the steps towards us. One opened the door, poked her head into the car. She stared first at Razz, then at me. She was about my mum's age, tall with close-cropped mousy hair and bright strawberry-field lipstick.

'Kari?' she said.

I looked at Razz, then at Jake. This was something I couldn't get my head round. Everywhere I went someone knew my name.

Jake raised his eyebrows and shrugged at me. So did Razz.

The woman held out her hand. 'I'm Chris. I work here. I've been looking forward to meeting you.'

'Yeah?' I ignored her hand. 'You can tell us what's going on then?'

She frowned. 'Haven't they told you anything?'

I shook my head. 'No.'

124

'It's about time someone told us something,' Jake said irritably.

Chris looked him up and down. 'Who's this?'

I told him. 'Razz is my friend too.'

Chris looked puzzled for a moment. Then she shrugged. 'They didn't tell me you'd be bringing friends. Oh, well, lack of communication as usual.' She spread out her hand. She had long, witch's nails and wore a gold ring on her little finger.

Zeon had got out and was standing behind her as I clambered out. I gave him a werewolf look. Razz and Jake came out behind me.

'I hope you're not hurt,' he said to me.

'Fat lot you care,' I said.

'Oh, but I do, Kari,' he said in a soft foxy voice. 'I care very much. And so do lots of other people.'

My stomach turned over when he said that. Supposing he told our parents where we were? Mum would kill me for lying to her and we would never be allowed out on our own again.

I shoved the thought to the back of my mind. I had the sneaking feeling Zeon didn't want *anyone* to know we were here. He didn't even want people to know HAPPY DAYS RETIREMENT HOME existed.

Which it didn't.

'Thanks, Mark,' Chris said to Zeon. 'I'm really grateful. You'll need to sign her over to me.'

'What?' I was beginning to feel more angry than scared. 'Sign who over to who?'

Chris put her hand on my shoulder. 'It's OK, Kari, it's just a formality.' She turned to Zeon. 'You haven't explained then?'

'I thought it was better left to you people.'

They touched fingertips. 'Yes. Thanks again,' Chris said. 'You've done a good job getting her here.'

'He didn't get me here,' I said indignantly. 'We came ourselves. We want to see Rachel.' *And take her home*, I added to myself.

'You'll see her very soon,' Chris said. When she said that my stomach gave a great kangaroo leap.

'She's really here, then?' Jake couldn't hide the relief in his voice. All along we hadn't known *definitely* that she would be.

'Yes,' Chris said. 'You can see her later when you've cleaned up and had something to eat. She'll be really pleased to see you.'

'Yeah, I bet she will,' Jake said. 'But we're not staying. We want to take her home with us.'

'I promise we'll look after her,' I blurted out. 'She won't need to be on the street—'

'It's all right,' Chris interrupted. 'She *is* being looked after.'

'But—'

Chris wouldn't say any more. 'I'll explain everything later,' was all she said. We exchanged looks again. If anyone else told us that we would probably erupt.

Chris beckoned to the other woman and introduced her. 'This is my colleague, Marion, you'll be seeing a lot of her too. She'll be helping me—'

' 'elping you what?' Razz narrowed his eyes at Marion.

But Chris was already going on ahead. She turned. 'Please follow me.'

I looked helplessly at Razz and Jake. If we wanted to see Rachel it was obvious we had no choice.

So we went up the steps with them and into the house. The door shut electronically behind us with a sinister dull thud. I could just imagine how a prisoner felt when his cell door clicked shut behind him.

Inside, we stared.

'Wow!' Razz gave a low whistle. 'What a place.'

A massive hall, high as a shopping mall. Ornately carved ceilings, a curving staircase leading up to the next floor. Masses of doors led off the hall. Through the glass of one I could see more people in lab coats. They were lounging around on overstuffed chairs and drinking out of white mugs and scoffing biscuits.

126

'A relic of a bygone age,' Chris said sharply when she saw us staring. 'Come on. I'll show you to your rooms.'

'Rooms?' Jake said.

'Blimey.' Razz was still looking amazed. 'Not an 'otel is it?'

Chris ignored him.

We dodged the house-robots hoovering the stairs and followed Chris. All the way up there were pale patches on the walls where royal portraits used to hang.

At the top, another robot came out of one of the rooms with a bundle of linen in its arms. It threw it on to a heap of others then went back inside.

We squeezed past and Chris opened a door on the left. 'This is your room, Kari,' she said. She took out her pocket PC and consulted it. 'There's a room free for you boys at the other end.'

'Blimey,' Razz said again. 'It *is* an 'otel.'

'It's no good,' I insisted. 'We're not staying. I told you, we're taking Rachel home.'

Chris said in a wheedling kind of voice. 'But I'm sure you'd like a wash and a change of clothes, Kari.'

I looked down at myself and decided she was right.

'We want to stay together,' Jake said.

I saw Chris's eyes suddenly glitter. She hadn't had any kind of aura that I could read but now I could see it, hovering a simmering dull impatient orange around her face. She pressed her lips together in a tight line, just like my mum did when she was angry. There was something about her too that I noticed for the first time. A kind of burning curiosity in her eyes when she looked at me. As if she was trying to see into my head but couldn't. She had an air of anxiety too. The same anxiety Zeon had that night he was searching for Rachel.

'Please do as I say.' She glanced at the boys, eyeing Jake's torn T-shirt. 'I'll send up some clothes for you too.'

I put my hand on Razz's arm. 'Go on,' I said. 'See you in ten minutes.'

Exactly seven minutes later I'd had a quick lick and a promise, brushed the tangles out of my hair and stuck on the grey sportsuit I'd found in my room. I didn't know how they knew my size but it fitted exactly. Trainers too.

Outside I almost collided with a man in green overalls collecting the bundles of dirty linen. He had *Next-day Linen Service* printed on his top pocket.

I squeezed past his trolley then whizzed along to the boys' room. They had already gone. Cursing them for not waiting for me I ran along the corridor. Then curiosity got the better of me and I opened a door to see what was inside.

It looked like someone's office. There was a computer and a huge star-map on the wall as well as a couch covered in a white sheet and some kind of electronic equipment. I went and had a closer look. I picked up a pair of electrodes that had wires attached to a machine with an LCD panel. I shuddered. It looked like some kind of ancient instrument of torture. I went out quickly and shut the door. In another room there were two more couches with big overhead lights that shone down on them. Everything was white and clinical—especially the glass cupboard in the corner full of drugs and hypos in plastic covers.

I couldn't get out of there fast enough. I ran out and whizzed down to the ground floor to look for Jake and Razz.

Down there, some of the rooms had names on their doors. Doctor Jeanne Chevalier, Doctor Sanjay Vermer, Professor Hans Schmidt. I opened one. There was a man sitting at a desk. He glanced up when I came in then called out when I fled.

I dived into another room. This one had Doctor Christine Evans on the outside.

On her desk was a stack of cardboard files.

I crept in and shut the door softly behind me. The screensaver on the computer was flinging hummingbirds at me as I sifted through the stack. There was a name on each one. Albert Sims, Jo-Anne Presley, Wayne Hudson, Gillian Coleman, Alan Marsden, and on the top . . . mine . . . Kari Charles.

I drew in my breath. Heart thudding I opened it up.

Daughter of Asia Brookner and George Charles, born 2034.

Reading through, my legs suddenly felt wobbly and I had to sit down. Why did they have my whole life history on file? Hair colour, eye colour, where I was born, how many kilograms I weighed. Where I lived, when I learned to read, when I first played the flute, how I had got lost when I was small. They'd even got my study progress grades, reports from my Link Tutor . . . everything.

Then my stomach suddenly knotted up. Got lost? I didn't remember that. At the top of the page I noticed a file reference. I turned to the computer, clicked on *file* and keyed it in.

It came up at once. The whole family history. Photos . . . me, a baby, a little kid . . . Mum, Dad, Damien . . . the Cottage. Everything. There were Newsnet headlines.

Well-known architect and designer George Charles sets up consultancy.

Terrorist shot near country cottage.

Lost girl turns up safe and well.

I stopped dead in my tracks and scanned the story.

Three-year-old Kari Charles, who had wandered away from her home, was found today. She was apparently none the worse for her adventure. Kari was discovered walking along a disused railway line near her home. She had been missing for three days.

'We never thought we would see her again,' Kari's mother, twenty-one-year-old Market Research Director, Asia Brookner, told Newsnet. 'But she's fine. Just a bit confused. Kari is a very inquisitive child and had probably gone exploring.' Ms Brookner looked pale from her ordeal.

'We've no idea where she has been,' she said, hugging Kari. *'We moved to the country so Kari would grow up away from the danger and pollution of the City,'* she added.

Kari, who is thought to be gifted musically, has been unable to explain where she has been.

There was another picture of me . . . a smiling red-haired kid in dungarees clutching a doll.

I leaned closer to the screen. My heart was thudding like a rockband and my palms were sweating. The doll. It was the same one I had found in the tunnel. No wonder it had given me a funny feeling. It was the doll I'd lost all those years ago.

I read it again. Had that child really been me? I ransacked my memory but nothing came up. Why had Mum never told me about it? The story made me feel really weird. As if I'd lived another life that I knew absolutely nothing about.

When the hummingbirds began flying at me again I turned in my chair and took another look at the desk folders. I opened another one. *Wayne Hudson. Born Euro 1996.* I keyed in his file code and opened it. What I read took away my breath. Wayne Hudson had lived a perfectly ordinary life until on January 6th, 2032 he had disappeared. He wasn't seen again until 2040 when he suddenly appeared back in his home town, confused and disorientated but none the worse for his experience. He had vague memories of lights and strange looking people but could tell no one where he had been.

There were hundreds of people like him all over the World. So Blenham *was* a kind of laboratory after all. A laboratory where they investigated people who, at some time in their lives, had mysteriously disappeared.

I sat back in the chair. The seed of an idea that had sown itself in my mind when I read my own file suddenly sprouted and grew until it was a great big tree of disbelief and fear.

Heart thudding, I quickly hunted through the pile for

Rachel's folder. It could tell me things about her past that would answer a lot of questions. But, strangely, it wasn't there.

Then the door opened and Chris came in.

I whirled round guiltily. She stared at me for a second or two then closed the door behind her. She pulled up another chair and sat down beside me.

'You've found your file?'

'Yes,' I said. I shook my head. 'I don't understand . . . '

My hand was still shaking as Chris took it into her own and rubbed it, just as Rachel had done that night when we were gazing at Starlight City. She drew a deep breath.

'OK, Kari,' she said. 'I'd better tell you.'

12

What Chris told me made my mind spin even more. I
didn't believe her at first. I thought it was just one of
those tales you read about on the tabloid Newsnet. I'd
scanned a few of them when I'd been surfing through
Timescan. UFOs, abductions, out-of-body experiences.
But *me* . . . and Rachel . . . and all those others. Others
who had mysteriously lost chunks of their lives that
they'd never been able to explain.

Like I apparently had.

It was crazy, stupid, a fairy tale . . .

In the middle of it all I got up and headed for the
door.

'I'm not listening,' I yelled. 'You're making it all up.
I'm going to see Rachel, she'll tell me it isn't true. This
is just a place where you do experiments on people and I
want to go home.'

But half-way to the door, I stopped. It was no good—
I *had* to hear the rest.

I sat down and suddenly exploded into tears. I
couldn't help it. What she told me had curdled my
brain.

She watched me for a second or two then coolly
handed me a tissue from the box in her drawer. She
waited while I sobbed then blew my nose, then sniffed
and stopped. I flashed her a bright red glare then sat
fiddling with the soggy tissue, tearing bits off and letting
them drop on the floor.

'And so you see, Kari,' she went on calmly as if the
whole World hadn't just turned completely upside

down, 'we've been following your progress ever since that time you went missing. We've got thousands of files on people like you. People who are never seen again, people whose dead bodies are found. People who turn up. Those who come back . . . If we manage to locate them we bring them here to try to help them remember where they've been and what's happened to them. It's difficult to find out exactly who's telling the truth and who is either mentally unbalanced or simply making things up. But we've got ways of finding out.'

'Yeah,' I said. 'I bet you have.' Alarm bells had begun donging in my head. A picture of all that electronic stuff, the couches, the drug cabinets, invaded my brain.

She leaned closer. 'Kari, we simply talk to them. We use hypnosis—' she broke off.

I stood up, pushing my chair back, suddenly more scared than I'd ever been in my life. 'I'm out of here,' I said.

She threw out her arm to stop me. 'Kari, you must realize that we have to find out the truth. The future of the whole human race could be at stake.'

I had my hand on the doorknob. 'You're crazy, all of you. Paranoid.'

'No, Kari. Look, I can show you hundreds more files.' She leaned forward and keyed in a code. A list came up on the screen. She scrolled through. Loads and loads.

'Kari,' she said. 'We know they're here . . . somewhere.'

'Who?'

'The people you were with when you went missing. The ones who have been taking people away then sending them back when they've finished with them.'

I went back to the chair and sat down heavily. 'You don't mean *aliens*?'

She looked at me. 'Yes, Kari. That's exactly what I do mean.'

I gazed at her in chronic disbelief. 'You've got to be joking.'

She shook her head. 'No, Kari.'

And suddenly I could see she was telling the truth. And when I saw that, suddenly, with a mighty, thunderous crash, some more pieces of the puzzle fell smartly into place.

My dream figures in the tunnel . . . the ones who came out of the bright light towards me. They had been Jon and the Others. I *knew* I had seen some of them before. I closed my eyes and seemed to see them again. Coming, hands outstretched, towards me. No wonder they had seemed so huge . . . I had only been three years old.

I realized Chris was still rattling on although I hardly heard what she was saying. My brain seemed to have gone into standby mode and my hands were shaking so much I had to sit on them.

'We need you to help us,' she was saying. She leaned forward again and held up one hand, clicking her fingers together. There was an intense almost manic gleam in her eyes. 'We're *that* close,' she said.

My heart was thumping so crazily I could hardly speak. They were a lot closer than they realized.

'We've *got* to find them, Kari,' she said.

'Are they here, then?' I said. 'On our World?'

'Yes,' she said. She took a deep breath and managed to calm herself down. 'When you were found you weren't in any distress as any other missing child would have been. You were warm, clean, happy, and had been fed.'

'I could have been at someone's house,' I interrupted.

She shook her head. 'No. All your neighbours were interrogated. No one had sheltered you. It was wintertime and there had been no cars through the area toll-booths that week; only those belonging to your family and neighbours.'

'Oh,' I said.

'And you talked about your friends from the light but couldn't explain what you meant. Almost everyone who has disappeared and been returned has said the same. Some remember more than others.'

I shook my head. 'But I don't remember anything,' I lied. 'I didn't even *know* I'd wandered off.'

'No. And your parents wouldn't allow you to be questioned.'

I swallowed. 'What about Rachel?'

Chris looked cagey.

'We're not sure about Rachel,' she said. 'She was just reported as appearing suddenly near your house and when we checked our files to find out who lived there we found we had one on you.'

I was so bewildered I thought my brain would burst. 'But I'd never met Rachel before.'

'No,' Chris said. 'But we always pick up people found in those kind of circumstances.'

'Drifters?' I said.

She nodded. 'Misfits, addicts, everyone found wandering. We've got several establishments.'

'What? Happy Days Retirement Homes,' I scoffed.

'We've got a variety of cover names,' she said icily.

'Who reported her?' I asked.

Chris gazed at me. 'We've got people everywhere.'

There was such a veiled kind of menace in her voice that I suddenly went cold. It was as if a ghost had flitted over my skin. Jon . . . the Others . . . they were in more danger than they realized. We *had* to warn them before it was too late.

'Has she told you anything?' I asked.

Chris shook her head. 'No, not yet. And we haven't got a file on her but we feel there's some kind of connection between the two of you. Otherwise, why would you have gone to such lengths to help her?'

I shrugged. It was a question I couldn't answer.

'I just didn't want her to be hurt,' I said but I knew it sounded pretty lame. There *was* a connection between me and Rachel but I had no real idea what it was.

'We're going to try to help you remember,' Chris was saying.

I stood up again. 'I want to see Rachel,' I said.

Chris stood up too. 'Right,' she said. 'We're going to start your interviews in the morning so I want you to get a good night's rest.'

'Where are Razz and Jake?'

'They're being interviewed at the moment,' she said.

'They don't know anything.'

She smiled. 'Just in case. Now, I'll take you to Rachel.'

We went up the stairs and along the corridor. At the end was a massive oak door with *Solar* written on it. Beside it was an empty laundry trolley. Chris almost tripped over it. She clicked her tongue.

'These trolleys are supposed to be kept in the basement,' she said. 'Someone's going to fall over one and break their neck.'

She took her mobile out of her pocket and punched in a number. She gave orders for the trolley to be moved, then opened the door and ushered me in.

The long, sunny room must have stretched almost the whole length of the great house. There were rows of beds beneath a heavily ornate ceiling. I stood on the threshold, frowning.

'What's this? It looks like a medi-centre.'

'Some of our visitors are poorly when they arrive,' she said. 'We put them here and nurse them back to health.'

'Where are they, then?' My brain was whirling again. 'And where's Rachel? She wasn't ill?'

'No, but she's quite frail,' Chris said. 'A lot of our people are—'

'She wasn't,' I insisted. A sudden fear was turning me to ice. I remembered how strong she was. How she had strode up the embankment towards the tunnel as if she was an athlete. 'What have you done to her?'

'Nothing.' Chris led me past the rows of beds. 'Come and see.'

The room adjoining was sunny too. It faced west and the afternoon sun warmed it like a furnace. There was a table in the middle radiant with a huge vase of flowers.

More comfy chairs, in a semi-circle in front of a wide bay window and a wall lined with leather-bound books. A figure was standing in front of the window gazing out over the wilderness that used to be the garden. The sunlight made her hair look like an outburst of thistledown round her head.

As we went in, heads turned to stare at us.

Then someone said, 'Rachel, she's here.'

The figure at the window spun round. I hesitated for just a second then ran straight into her arms.

'Kari, I'm so sorry,' was the first thing she said.

'Tell me none of this is true,' I said.

She held me at arm's length and gazed at me. 'I'm sorry,' she said again.

I looked round but Chris had gone.

'Rachel.' I said it in a low voice so none of the others could hear. 'We've got to help them . . . your friends at *Starhost.*'

She looked startled for a brief second. Then she said, 'You found them, then?'

'Yes.'

They allowed me to talk to Rachel for an hour before they came to take me away. It was just long enough for me to tell her everything that had happened.

There was still no sign of Razz and Jake.

'I want to know they're OK,' I insisted as Chris took me back down the stairs.

She laughed. 'They're perfectly all right. Did you think we were going to torture them?'

'It wouldn't surprise me,' I said.

And then I spotted them. They were in the staff lounge, sprawled out in the armchairs in front of the TV scoffing burger and chips.

Chris opened the door for me. The room was empty except for the two boys. 'Not too long, now,' she said. 'Don't forget we want you to get that good night's sleep.'

Just then, I didn't think I'd ever sleep again.

Before I said anything, I went and turned the TV up really loud.

'Rachel says all the rooms are bugged,' I hissed.

We settled ourselves near the set.

'OK,' I said in a low voice. 'What happened?'

'They just kept asking questions,' Jake told me. 'Mostly about why you and I had come here, what we'd been up to, that kind of stuff.'

'What did you tell them?'

'Nothing.' He grinned.

'They knew we were looking for Rachel,' I said.

'I reckon they spotted us together then lost us,' Razz said. He grinned. 'I know that place like the back of me hand. Then when they spotted me on me own they followed me back. I told 'em I didn't know nothing about you. Just that you was two country kids got lost. Then we'd split and that was that.'

'Do you think they believed you?' I asked.

He wiped the back of his hand across his mouth. Then he shrugged.

'Dunno. I told 'em I often went out to the Stairs— ghost hunting. They think I'm barmy.'

I chuckled. 'Ghost hunting?'

'Yeah,' he said. 'People say it's haunted out there.'

And then I told them what had happened to me.

I didn't think they would believe me. Strangely, though, they did.

Razz shook his head. 'I knew there was something really weird about that place,' he said sounding dazed. 'That Jon bloke . . . he just appeared from nowhere. And you couldn't see nuffin' from the outside. I don't know how they done it.'

As for Jake, it was as if all his dreams had come true.

When at last he'd got his breath back and could speak, he said, 'We've got to get out of here, Kari. We've got to warn them.'

My heart turned over. 'I know,' I said. And then I

told them about a plan I'd hatched when I was talking to Rachel.

At first they burst out laughing. Razz snorted bits of burger all over the place. 'That'll never work,' he scoffed. 'You've been watching too many of them fantasy flicks.'

I leaned close to him. 'It will work,' I hissed. 'It's got to.'

'We could send 'em one of them e-messages,' Razz said suddenly.

'No,' Jake said quickly. 'They'll know if we use their machines. You can bet your life they'll be monitoring everything we do. That's why the rooms are bugged.'

'That's what Rachel said,' I told them. 'We've got to get back to *Starhost* and tell them ourselves.'

13

Before I went to bed I ran up to see Rachel again.

I opened the Solar door and crept in. The room was in semi-darkness. Some people were reading by the light of tiny halogens above their heads. Some were just lying there listening to their pocket stereos.

'Kari?' A voice behind me made me jump. 'What are you doing?'

I turned to see a woman sitting just behind the door. She had a laptop on her knees, the screen covered in notes.

'I . . . I wanted to say goodnight to Rachel,' I fibbed.

She indicated a bed by the window. 'Don't be long and don't disturb the others,' she said.

I flashed her a smile. 'Thanks.' I tried to sound calm and hoped I'd fooled her.

I tiptoed over to Rachel. She was lying on her back wide awake, gazing at the ceiling. 'Kari!' Her face flooded with pleasure when she saw me.

I took her hand and held my finger to my lips. It only took a few minutes to whisper our plan.

'There's guards everywhere,' she said.

'I know. But we don't care. We've got to get out before they make us tell them.'

'Yes,' she said. 'Their methods don't work with me . . . just weaken me a little, but you, Kari—'

The warden or guard or whatever she was, came to tell me to go. 'Don't worry,' I whispered quickly to Rachel. 'It'll be OK. I'll see you in the morning.'

She smiled. 'OK.'

In bed, I lay for ages, my brain whirlpooling around. I was petrified of what they were going to do to me. The thought of some hypnotist probing my subconscious gave me the shudders. Taking me back to a time in my childhood that I hadn't even known existed. And if I betrayed Jon and the Others I knew I would never forgive myself. I couldn't bear to think what the government might do to people like them.

Before I'd gone to bed, I'd looked out of the window. The night was clear, the stars so huge and close you felt you could almost touch them. I wondered where *they* had come from. Somewhere up there in Starlight City. No wonder Rachel had looked at it with such a strange expression on her face. She told me they had sent her to find me. To see how I had grown up in the years since they *borrowed* me. She said they didn't ever keep anyone against their will and I had been too little to decide whether I wanted to stay with them or not.

I wondered what their life was like on their far distant world. What its name was. What the colour of their sky was. I wished I could go there to see. People reckoned aliens would be monsters or lizards with tails and claws. But they weren't—they were just like us.

A knock on my door next morning woke me from a restless sleep. I'd had the dreams again. The one with the people coming towards me out of the light. But this time I knew exactly who they were.

The door opened and Marion came in with a mug of tea.

I groaned and rolled over. It was time to put the first part of our scheme into action.

Marion put the mug on the bedside table. 'How are you feeling, Kari?'

'Terrible.' I groaned and put my hand on my forehead. 'I've got a terrible headache.'

Marion frowned. 'I'll get you a shot of pain killer.'

I shook my head, still groaning. 'It won't do any

good. It's a migraine. I get them a lot.' I struggled to sit up. 'I think I'm going to be sick.'

I thrust back the covers and ran into the bathroom. I closed the door and made sick noises over the loo. I splashed my face with water and staggered out.

'I'm sorry,' I said.

'I'll get one of the medics to come and see you.' Marion sat on the bed, stroking my forehead.

'I'll be OK,' I said. 'I just need to sleep.'

Chris came later. With her was a man with a deep voice.

I didn't open my eyes. I heard them talking in low tones. Then I felt a hand on my shoulder and Chris said, 'Let me give you an injection, Kari. You'll feel better in no time.'

'It won't do any good,' I groaned into the pillow. 'Nothing does.'

I knew if I really had been sick and it was the same medication we kept at home, it would cure me instantly.

Chris sighed. 'It looks as if we'll have to leave her until later,' she said and they went out.

I lay motionless, scared they would come back. When I decided it was safe, I got up and dressed quickly. I rearranged the bedclothes, stuffing the pillows down under the sheets so it looked as if I was still in there. Then I sat by the window and waited.

Half an hour later I saw the linen service van come whirring up the drive. It disappeared round the back.

I dodged out into the corridor and ran to the boys' room. Inside they were waiting for me. They had been watching for the van too. Our theory that *Next-day Laundry Service* really meant what it said had turned out to be right.

'Did you locate the basement stairs?' I asked Razz.

'Yep.' He grinned. Jake handed me a bit of paper. He'd drawn a map on it. A map of the maze of Blenham's corridors. He pointed. 'Look, down here, through the kitchens and down the staircase at the end.'

142

'You go first and if anyone stops you, you're lost, OK?' Jake reminded me. 'And try to look confused.'

'That won't be hard.' I flashed him a grin and went out.

Rachel was already there. Hovering by the kitchen door. We hugged one another silently then went in. The kitchen didn't look as if anyone had used it for years. A massive black antique cooker stood inside the fireplace. In the centre was a long table strewn with old pots and pans dull and grimy from neglect.

'They use another room,' Rachel explained.

'Lucky for us,' I said.

We went down into the basement. It was used as a storeroom. Boxes of dehydrated food, shelves lined with packets, racks of wine and mineral water. Two enormous freezers rumbled against one wall. And at the end, double doors led outside to the delivery area.

They suddenly opened and a man appeared. He wheeled in a trolley full of clean linen. Then he went back for another. Eventually he had unloaded the van. He looked at his watch then took a pack of cigarettes out of his pocket and sat down on the floor. He lit up and sat there puffing as if he had all the time in the World before taking the laundry through the old kitchen and into the house.

Rachel and I had dodged down behind a stack of boxes. My heart drummed. Where were Razz and Jake, they should have been right behind us?

Then Razz appeared. Before I'd had a chance to warn him, he sauntered coolly down the aisle between the shelves. If he was shocked to see someone sitting there he didn't show it.

'Wotcha, mate,' he breezed. 'Know where they keep the . . . er . . . software?'

The man shrugged. 'How should I know?'

Razz raised his eyebrows. 'Just thought you might.' He began looking at the boxes, standing on tiptoe to try to see the ones higher up.

As he turned the corner he spotted us crouched down on the floor. He grinned and winked at us then disappeared again.

'I reckon they're up there, mate,' he said. 'Couldn't give me a hand, could you?'

The man made an impatient sound. 'There's a ladder somewhere.' Reluctantly, he helped Razz look for it. We heard a clang, the man swear, and Razz apologize.

'Sorry, mate. You 'urt?' He didn't sound sorry at all.

I stared at Rachel. What was Razz up to? And where was Jake? If he didn't turn up soon it would be too late. Eventually we heard the squeak of the trolley wheels and the man trundled it along the aisle next to us and disappeared into the kitchen.

I leapt up. 'Where's Jake?'

'Here,' said a voice behind us.

Later, when we were safely aboard *Jetstream*, he explained what he had been doing. I'd thought it was a stroke of luck that the van had conked out just beyond sight of the gate.

'Don't be daft,' Jake said. 'I fixed it.'

I really didn't know how we'd managed to get out safely. First there had been a house-robot who came to carry out a carton of dried food. It spotted us straight away.

'Good morn—' was all it had time to say before Jake de-activated it. Hopefully it hadn't had a chance to log us into its memory.

Then there had been the one who came to get a new supply of polish just before the van operator came back with a trolley of dirty linen. Luckily it didn't bat a metal eyelid when we told it we were helping out with the laundry.

'Hope it doesn't run a check,' Jake said.

When the operator had swapped trolleys we bundled Rachel into one and covered her with the sheets.

Then we heard him whistling as he came back with the final one.

'Quick!' Jake shoved me into another trolley. I covered myself up.

Jake and Razz squeezed themselves into the remaining trolley. Microseconds later, the man appeared with the last trolley of dirty linen. Whistling, he began to load up.

I heard him grunt as he pushed the boys' trolley up the slope. At the top he bent to examine the wheels. Then he got out his pocket PC and keyed something in.

He loaded the other trolleys, slammed the van doors shut, and we were on our way.

Over the top of the engine's whirr I heard someone shouting. I squeezed my eyes shut tight and didn't dare breathe. But we didn't stop. We just whirred towards the barrier. I heard the window slide down. There was one heart-stopping moment when someone banged their fist on the roof, then we were off again, trundling down the drive until there was suddenly a grating noise and we ground to a halt. The driver swore loudly and got out. He lifted the seat to look at the cells.

It had been then that we clambered out and ran to hide in the undergrowth until he got the van going again and drove off.

When he'd gone we danced around, hugging one another and whooping like mad. Rachel just stood there, pale and unsmiling.

'Right,' I said when we'd sobered up 'Let's go.'

Razz was looking round in panic. 'Where's the bloomin' boat?'

When we'd all clambered aboard, Rachel said, 'Do you think we should wait until dark?' She was sitting in the cabin, pulling leaves and bits of bramble out of her hair and trying to get her breath back.

'No.' Jake was already fiddling around, desperately trying to get the engine started. 'We'd be stopped by the patrols. If we go now we'll just blend in with the rest.'

So that's what we did. When Jake finally got the engine going we untied the ropes and set off.

Razz sat on the top, acting as lookout. We were still scared they *would* come after us. It seemed too good to be true that no one had spotted us.

'Can't you go no faster?' he shouted to Jake.

'No,' Jake shouted back. 'We'll attract too much attention.'

But there was only the usual river traffic chugging up and down. No one took any notice of a tatty old boat cruising gently downriver as if it was just out for a day's jaunt.

Rachel and Razz hid in the cabin when we stopped at the marina to fill up with fuel.

When we set off again Razz came on deck and I went down into the cabin to talk to Rachel.

There were a million questions I wanted to ask her.

'How long did *you* stay with . . . them?' I couldn't bring myself to call them *aliens*. Aliens made them sound as if they were something horrible and scary.

She smiled a far-away smile. 'Ooh, a long time.'

'What did they do to you?'

'Do to me?' She laughed. 'You've been reading too many tabloid tales.'

'Well, why did they want you, then? Did they pick you at random or did they choose you specially?'

'Like they did you, Kari?'

I frowned. 'Did they choose me specially?'

'Oh, yes,' she said.

I was just about to ask her how Jon had always managed to seem to appear out of nowhere when Razz came rattling down the stairs. She hadn't answered anything properly. She was just like Jon, both a whizz at evading questions.

'There's a bleedin' patrolboat hailing us,' Razz told us breathlessly.

I looked around in panic. 'You'd better hide.'

He shrugged. 'Where? You can't swing a cat round in 'ere.'

146

But somehow or other they managed to stuff themselves into the cupboards beneath the bunks in the stern.

It was the same launch that had stopped us on the way upstream.

'How was your auntie?' the woman asked. She didn't even bother to come on board when she saw it was us. 'Bought you new sportsuits, did she?'

'Er . . . yeah,' Jake croaked.

She grinned and passed back our cards, said something to the driver, and they swung away, the sleek hull carving a white arrow of foam as they gathered speed and disappeared out of sight.

I waved. 'See you next vacation!'

Then Jake looked at me and we burst into giggles of relief.

The sun had set by the time we arrived back at the Stairs. The water had grown black with the darkening sky. It looked thick as treacle as we came alongside the steps and Razz jumped ashore with the rope.

We helped Rachel clamber out.

Jake was looking thoughtful.

I stared at him. 'What's wrong?'

He shook his head. 'It was too easy,' he said.

'What do you mean?' Rachel pulled the edges of her cardigan together against the cool evening breeze.

Jake bit his lip. 'Just what I say. All that security and we got away . . . '

'In that case,' Razz said—he had pulled his cart from the cockpit and yanked it up the steps—'we'd better warn them . . . fast.'

It seemed our feet hardly touched the ground as we hurried along the river road. We skirted the rubbish tips and ran through the wharves and the waterhouses to the bombed-out office buildings.

Moonshadows cast spells across the fountain and the cobblestones as we got to the square. I squinted upwards. As usual there was no sign of anyone. A flock of birds rose from the branches of a dead tree and flew away into the darkness with a wild panic-stricken beating of wings. We just stood there, looking up . . . waiting helplessly.

Razz began pacing up and down. 'Come *on*, mate!'

Fed up, Jake went over to the door. 'I'm going in.'

I ran after him. But then we saw the door was half hanging off. There was a squeak and a scrabbling of claws and a rat ran out between Jake's feet and scampered away.

He stepped inside and stood at the bottom of the stairs. I followed.

'It's no good, Kari.' Jake was telling me something I already knew. 'They've gone.'

Then, in the far distance, we heard the unmistakable sound of a helicopter drumming its way across the City rooftops.

'The night patrol!' Jake said.

Razz cocked his head, listening. 'No, it's a different one. I reckon it's—'

We stared at one another in horror.

'Zeon!' Jake said. 'I was right. It *was* too easy.'

'But how—?' Razz began.

'Trackers, I bet,' Jake said. He began tearing off his jacket. 'These clothes . . . we must have been crazy not to guess.'

It only took us minutes to find them. Minutes when the hammersound of the helicopter got closer and closer.

Jake's had been attached to the back of one of the pocket studs on his jacket. Mine in the hem at the bottom of one of the trouser legs, Razz's was tucked into his waistband.

'Give 'em to me.' Razz grabbed them and ran out. He dodged through the alley and disappeared. Minutes later he was back. Grinning. 'Chucked 'em in the river,' he said. 'They'll think we've gone for a swim. Come on, let's scarper.'

We ran after him. At the end of the alleyway, he was

clambering up into the skip. He knelt on the edge and held his hand out for Rachel, close behind. 'Hurry!' he urged.

She put her foot on the ledge and hopped up like a two year old.

We buried ourselves under the rubbish with only microseconds to spare.

The helicopter landed in the square. We heard its blades slicing the air as it hovered for a second or two then settled. We lay still as stones, eyes closed, not daring to breathe.

It must have been an hour before they finally took off again. We heard shouting, crashes and bangs. And one voice above all. The one we were afraid we would hear . . . Zeon.

Razz crept out first, dodging down, skirting the alley, peering round the corner to make sure they hadn't left anyone on guard. By the light of the moon I saw him stand up, then beckon to us. The coast was clear.

'You know,' I said, 'they didn't *really* want us at all. They were just going to use us as a means of finding *Starhost*.'

'That's all they wanted any of us for,' Rachel said in a quiet voice.

Razz headed for the door. 'Come on, let's take a look.'

It was obvious where Zeon and his men had been. Stacks of rubbish tossed aside, footprints scuffed in the dust. But they had found nothing because there wasn't anything to find.

Every room was empty. The smashed windows, the broken furniture were just as you would imagine in a bomb-blasted place. Among a pile of scorched papers lay an empty cigarette carton. The ones Zeon smoked. We couldn't help chuckling with glee when we found it. All the boxes, all the machines had gone. The slatted blinds clicked and rattled in the wind as we went from room to room then finally, cautiously up to the penthouse.

There was no sign that anyone had ever been there. The only things that walked there now were the ghosts.

I stood in the centre of the penthouse room. 'I don't understand,' I said. 'How could they have got out so quickly?'

When Rachel heard me ask that she came over and explained about the machines they had that split things into molecules, transported them from the ground to their ship, then reassembled them. They could do it with people too.

'Blimey,' Razz said.

'Umm.' Jake looked thoughtful. 'Yes, I can see how that's possible.'

I laughed and punched his shoulder. 'Of course it's possible, they did it, didn't they?'

'Why didn't they do it straight away?' Razz had been looking thoughtful. 'Like when they first suspected *Starhost* might be being watched.'

'The ship had gone to study another part of the galaxy,' Rachel said. 'They had to send a message then wait until it came back.' She smiled. 'Travelling through space takes a bit of time, you know.'

'Oh . . . I see,' Razz said in a voice that sounded as if he didn't see at all.

'I'm glad they've gone,' I said. 'If they had been discovered it would have been our fault.'

'No,' Rachel shook her head. 'It wasn't your fault. They knew they were close to being discovered. They knew it was time for them to go home.'

We all stared up through the glass roof as if we expected to see a starship warp across our vision. I glanced at Rachel. The moonlight reflected a kind of yearning on her face. I felt sorry for her. I remembered hearing her play the piano. She was a musician too. I had told her about playing with Jon and the Others. I imagined I could hear the echo of the music we made together. She told me she would have loved to have been there too.

150

Razz came to sit next to me on the floor. He must have seen how sad I looked.

He put his arm round me. 'Cheer up, Kari,' he said. 'I'll take you back to the terminal tomorrow and you can go 'ome.'

'Thanks for everything, Razz,' I said. 'I don't know what we would have done without you.'

He went red. I could see it, even though moonlight was all we had.

We all slept the night in the penthouse. Curled up on the floor all together to keep warm. Half asleep, I heard the music again . . . the soaring ghost-notes of the *Starhost* symphony. I knew I would never forget the time I'd played with them. It was the best time of my life and I felt so sad I thought my heart would break.

Rachel must have known what I was thinking. She felt for my hand and squeezed it.

'At least they're safe,' she said.

When I turned my head I could see starlight reflected in the sadness of her eyes.

'Yes,' I said. And I knew in my heart that was really all that mattered.

PART FOUR

Back Home

14

Razz took us back as far as the tram-link terminal. I
wanted him to come home with us but he wouldn't.

'Your dad would go bonkers,' he laughed. I'd already
told him how Dad reacted when Mum brought Rachel
home.

'I don't care.' I didn't think I could bear never to see
him again.

He put his hands on my shoulders. 'We're different
Worlds, me and you, Kari. Just as different as Jon and
all them people at *Starhost*.'

'But they were the same as us,' I said.

He looked at me, gazing into my eyes as if he could
see right into my mind. I could see a purple ring of
misery hovering above his head.

'No,' he said. 'They wasn't the same as us at all and I
ain't the same as you.'

I stared at him. He was right. On the surface we were
the same but that was about all. But meeting Rachel and
Razz had taught me one thing above all. That you could
never tell what people were like just by looking at them.

'Where shall we send the money?' I asked.

He frowned. 'What money?'

'The money we owe you for helping us.'

Razz shook his head. 'Forget it,' he said.

'But . . . '

I could see it was no good arguing so I didn't. Instead
I put my arms round him and hugged him. I buried my
face in the angle between his neck and his shoulder. I
felt his breath in my hair. His heart . . . my heart . . . his

groan as he bent his head and closed his eyes on the world that lay between us. Then he pushed me away, distancing himself from me but keeping his hands on my shoulders. His Adam's apple bounced up and down as he swallowed. His eyes were bright.

'They're waiting,' he said.

And when I looked, Jake and Rachel were watching us. Jake was pretending not to but I could see him peeping at us from under his eyelashes.

'Please come,' I said.

Razz let me go and shook his head. He grinned. 'No ID,' he said. 'As far as your world's concerned, I don't exist.'

'You exist in my world,' I whispered. 'You always will.'

Then he leaned forward and kissed me. 'Don't forget me, Kari.'

'I won't,' I said.

My eyes blurred as he turned and walked away.

Rachel held out her arm as he went past. They left Jake and stood together, talking. I saw Razz grin then throw back his head and laugh. Then he waved once. The crowd folded around him and he disappeared from sight.

Rachel came back to us. 'It's time for me to go too.'

I looked at her in horror. 'No, you're coming back with us.'

She shook her head gravely. 'No, Kari.'

My eyes flew about in panic. I grabbed Jake's arm.

'Tell her, Jake, tell her she's got to.'

But Jake just said, 'We can't make her if she doesn't want to.'

'It's not that,' Rachel said. 'I don't want to put you in any more danger. Zeon will come and find you again, Kari . . . make no mistake.'

'I don't care,' I said. 'I won't betray you.'

She smiled. 'I know but I want you and your family to be safe.'

'But where will you go?'

'Don't worry about me,' she said. 'I'll be all right. Honestly.'

I didn't understand anything. It was like the whole thing was starting over again. A circle. With me and Jake and Rachel being spun round and round and never finding any answers.

'Kari,' Jake said gently. 'I think we should get home. Our alibi isn't going to last for ever.'

'But we can't just leave Rachel here.' I made up my mind I wasn't going to budge until she agreed to come home with me.

Through the other side of the barrier I could see a tram glide in and disgorge its passengers. Its return destination flashed up on the screen. Jake glanced up.

'We've got to get through Security. Please, Kari.'

Rachel hugged me then gave me a slight push. 'Go on.'

'But . . . '

I realized it was no good arguing so we left her there. I could see her tall figure. She was standing upright, one hand on the steel rail. With the light behind her she looked like that warrior-queen I'd seen on the embankment the night they took her away.

'*Mind the doors, mind the doors,*' the robot voice droned.

They hissed shut and the tram slid away into the tunnel. The darkness folded in behind us and Rachel was gone.

I didn't speak all the way back. Jake was rattling on but I hardly heard a word he was saying. I felt as deflated as a popped balloon although I didn't really know why. We had done what we set out to do. We had found Rachel's friends . . . we had found *Rachel* and rescued her from Blenham. *And* we had met people from another world. That had to be the most fantastic, mind-boggling, freaking-out thing to ever happen to anyone. But still there was something missing.

There was still a gap in that puzzle and I knew I could never be truly happy again until it was filled.

'How's Vinny?' was the first thing Mum said to me when I arrived back.

Jake had gone home. He said his mum probably hadn't realized he'd even been away but he wanted to go home to change his clothes. I wasn't surprised. His odd assortment of sportsclothes had really taken a beating. A jagged hole where he had ripped out the bug. Engine oil all over the top, and the bottoms looked as if he'd slept in them for a week.

'Oh . . . she's great,' I said in answer to Mum's question.

She gave me one of her puzzled looks. 'Did you buy a new sportsuit?'

'Oh . . . er . . . yeah. Like it?'

'It's got a bit mucky,' Mum said. 'And torn. Give it to Archie to mend and put in the wash.'

'Yes, OK,' I said.

Mum sighed. 'What did you get up to?'

I shrugged. 'Nothing much. Went to the games centre, that kind of stuff.'

'Was Vinny's dad there?'

'No.'

'She was glad of the company then?'

'Yes.'

Mum sighed. She hates me answering in monosyllables but what else could I say?

I was leaning up against the doorway to her office. It was on the tip of my tongue to ask her about that time I went missing but before I could say anything she opened her desk drawer and took something out. The doll.

She turned to face me. 'I found this in your room,' she said. She touched its face with her fingertip and I saw a blue haze of emotion hovering around her head. 'Where did you find it?'

Then she gazed at me with one of those dragon looks that made it fatal for me to lie.

So I told her the truth.

'What were you doing up there? It's really dangerous.'

'We wondered if Rachel left any of her things behind, that's all.'

She stared at me for a minute. 'Did she?'

I shook my head and told another fib. 'No.'

'Poor Rachel, I wonder what happened to her?'

'Yes,' I said. 'I wonder.' My heart did a somersault. Rachel . . . alone and friendless in the City . . . what *was* going to happen to her?

'I really wanted to help her, you know,' Mum said.

'Yes.' I put my hand on her shoulder. 'I know.'

'This . . . ' Mum held up the doll. 'It was yours, you lost it when you were little. Do you remember?'

'I'm not sure,' I said.

She seemed satisfied with that. Maybe she had forgotten how scared she had been when I wandered off. Perhaps in a few years I'll forget how scared I'd been at Blenham. Maybe I'd forget Jon . . . the Others . . .

Somehow, though, I doubted it.

I went into my Dad's room, said 'Hi' and gave him a hug. He probably hadn't even noticed I'd been away.

He turned in his chair, surprised.

'Kari, what's up?'

'Nothing,' I said. 'I'm just glad to be home.'

'Home?'

I grinned. 'Forget it, Dad.'

He shrugged and went back to his screens.

In my room I took my flute out of its box. I drew a chair up to the window and sat looking out. I put the flute to my lips and began to play. It came so easily . . . the melody from the symphony I had played at *Starhost*. I played it over and over. The notes seemed to hang in the air for a minute or two then they rose up through the ceiling and out into the starry sky. Wherever Jon and the Others were, I hoped they could hear them.

Eventually I put the flute down and went over to my machine. I logged on. I wanted to put the music on disk and mail it to Jake. The screen said there was an e-message waiting. The mail reader's face came up in its little box in the corner of the screen. I deleted it. I hate its silly voice. It's supposed to sound like a real person but I've never heard anyone speak like that.

Kari:
  We didn't want to leave without explaining. We know you're feeling confused and puzzled and we're sorry we couldn't say goodbye properly but it wasn't safe for us to stay any longer. We're sorry too that we didn't answer any of your questions. We thought it better for you not to know until we had gone. What you witnessed at *Starhost* was a kind of reunion. A gathering of some of the host of people we've met during our visits to your world. People we especially admired—people with a gift for music. That's why we wanted *you* there, Kari. You are a person with a special gift—a natural ability to make music, something you must have been born with to have shown us when you were only three years old that you could make an instrument sing. You had other gifts too. You could see colours and moods that others cannot see. You were unique, Kari—you still are. You see, Kari, our mission has been to study and record the races we've encountered on our expeditions through time and space. We hope that, one day, these records will be available for the whole universe to read and learn about people from other worlds. We were surprised when we first came to your World. It's remarkably like ours was in *our* twenty-first century and you are the only aliens

we've met who look exactly the same as we do. We also found, even though your civilization isn't yet very advanced, that we share many things. A love of music is one of those things. We hope that, one day, your World will be able to put aside violence and poverty, power and hatred, just as our world has and that you will be able to reach out and find *us* among the stars. By the time you read this, our friends from your World will be on their way back to their homes. Who knows, one day you might meet them again. There's a couple of things we've got to do before we finally leave. One is to thank you. When we borrowed you all those years ago, you freely and without fear shared your gifts with us. Our way of saying thanks is to compose a symphony for you. We've called it Starlight City. When you look up into your night-time sky, Kari, remember us.

I read the message again and again until it was imprinted for ever on my mind. When I managed to stop crying I keyed in Jake's website address and got him straight away. Then I e-mailed the message on to him.

Five minutes later he came through on the videophone. It was the first time I'd ever seen Jake near to tears.

'I wish we could tell Razz,' I said, sniffing.

'I've got the feeling he already knows,' Jake said.

Then I remembered, Razz and Rachel, heads together at the tram terminal. Jake was right. Razz already knew.

'Are you going to tell anyone?' Jake asked.

'No,' I said. 'I want it to be our secret. Us and all the other host.'

Jake's face split into a broad grin. 'Suits me. So if Zeon turns up again . . . ?'

'Tell him to get lost,' I said.

Then Jake said, 'But the piece they've written for you . . . where is it?'

'I don't know,' I said. 'Perhaps they'll mail it another time.'

'Hope so,' Jake said.

Later, I went out into the garden. I kept running Jon's letter over and over in my head. He said they had a couple of things to do before they left. One was send me the message of thanks. I wondered what the other one could be.

The night was warm, the air heavy with the threat of a storm. The City-glow lit up the horizon and in the distance I heard a rumour of thunder. Black clouds were congregating over the hills. They were hemmed with blood from the setting sun.

I sat on the garden seat and stared at nothing. I could hear Archie clattering around in the kitchen, Damien in his room zapping something or other.

Then, suddenly, the lights came on and I saw a figure at the gate. I knew who it was straight away.

I ran down the path and keyed in the code. When the gate opened I grabbed her hands and pulled her inside.

She didn't look like a Misfit any more. Or a Drifter. She wore a grey kind of trouser suit made of some silky material I'd never seen before. Her hair was scraped up on top of her head and delicate golden ear-rings swung from her ears.

'You came back!'

She took my hand and led me back to the seat. 'Just for a while, Kari. There's something I decided I had to tell you. And I've brought you this.'

She handed me a small box. When I opened it I saw a shining micro-disk. Written on the label were the words: *'Starlight City—a symphony for Kari.'*

'Play it when I've gone,' she said.

And then I listened to what she had to tell me. When she'd finished I stared at her. My eyes must have been full of disbelief because she smiled and said, 'Didn't you guess?'

I shook my head. 'I . . . I thought . . . ' And then I didn't know *what* I had thought. 'Why were you dressed like a raggy old woman?'

She smiled again. 'A mistake,' she said. 'I thought I wouldn't be noticed . . . instead it worked the other way round.'

I grinned. I remembered that first time I'd seen her. Dressed in that tatty old coat and scarf and looking for all the World as if she was a Misfit. Never again would I jump to conclusions like that.

'I was so horrible to you.' My voice cracked up as I said it.

She shook her head. 'No, you weren't.'

I looked at her. There were a million questions I wanted to ask but I knew there wasn't time. There was one thing, though . . .

'What's it like?' I said. 'Your World?'

She sighed. 'If I had a week,' she said, 'it wouldn't be time enough to tell you.' She fiddled with the ring on her finger. 'From space,' she went on, 'it looks like a bright swirling orb of beautiful greens and blues and white with the lands beneath. Continents, mountain ridges, the oceans . . . ' She looked at me and smiled. 'Who knows, one day you might see it for yourself.'

'What do you call it?'

She looked up again. 'Earth,' she said. Then she pointed to a bright, winking star amongst the snowdrift of the others. 'Look, there it is.'

I gazed at it. 'Earth . . . ' I said the strange word softly. 'Earth . . . '

'It's from an ancient word *Eorthe*,' she told me. 'It means simply *the world*.'

'What do you call *our* World?' I asked.

'We call it Altair,' she said.

'Oh,' was the only thing I could think of to say.

She stood up.

'Let me come with you,' I said.

She hesitated. 'All right.'

And so we went through the gate and across the road. We jumped the ditch and climbed the embankment and made our way along the line towards the tunnel. The night air was still heavy. The thunder was rolling closer. There was a sudden crack and lightning split the horizon in half. A quick, warm wind blew my hair across my face.

'You'd better hurry,' I said.

'It's all right.' She glanced up at the sky. 'In fact it's perfect.'

Even in the gloom I could see the hole Rachel had blasted through the wall when she was running from Zeon. I wished I could tell Damien I'd met an alien who had a real zapper but didn't think he would believe me if I did. However much he wanted to.

Rachel stood in front of it and held out her arms. I hugged her quickly then let her go. She looked up as another flash of lightning slashed across the sky.

'They're almost here,' she said.

I watched as she walked into the tunnel . . . a dark figure against the blinding light. Then, suddenly, she was gone.

I turned and ran all the way home.

Also by Sue Welford

The Shadow of August
ISBN 0 19 271595 X

'Mattie, you say your mum must have had a good reason to lie to you. Well, you're right, she did.'

When Mattie's mother dies, Mattie begins to discover that a lot of the things her mother had told her about her childhood weren't true after all. And the more Mattie tries to unravel her past, the more mysteries appear. Why had her mother never told her about the house in Cornwall? Why had she never met her grandparents? And who were the two figures who always seemed to be hovering on the edge of her life— just out of reach?

Eventually, Mattie feels that her whole existence is one big lie and that she can't be certain of anything.

'A convincing read—both plot and characters hold the reader's attention.'
Books for Keeps

'A first-class mystery—a junior Ruth Rendell.'
The Observer

'A gripping mystery.'
The Times

The Night After Tomorrow
ISBN 0 19 271726 X

January . . . the wolf month . . . wolf-monath . . .

Jess felt she had been broken to pieces. Nothing worked for her any more. So it was good to get away and find some space with her aunt in the country.

But the country wasn't quite as peaceful as she thought it would be. In the forest there were strange noises and movements. When Jess was in bed, there was the sense of someone or something outside, watching, waiting for her. On the farms, the cattle and sheep were being slaughtered by a savage creature—the forest beast they called it.

And then there was Luc, who seemed to belong to the wild, with his hypnotic amber-coloured eyes and long hair. Why was he so interested in the forest beast? Why had no one ever seen his mother? And what was it that could only be done the night after tomorrow?

'The ingredients of classic horror in this well-crafted and sensitive tale.'

Books for Keeps

'This is a good, strong novel.'
School Librarian

Charlie on the Spot
ISBN 0 19 271676 X

'Being almost fourteen's not all it's cracked up to be. Especially if you're a girl.'

Charlie has a lot of problems these days. Her mum is pregnant and has given up her job on the building site. Mum's partner, new-man Jed, is going to ante-natal classes and has started to suffer from morning sickness. And of course Mum has decided they're all going to move to the country.

Meanwhile, Mum has taken over the school pantomime which she thinks is sexist, cast Charlie as the policeperson, and showed Snow White how to defend herself from sexual harassment from the prince.

So, in the middle of all this, how is Charlie going to get the pair of spotted shoes she longs for? How is she going to become an actor? And above all, how is she going to get her first kiss from her alleged boy-friend, Gazza?

'An entertaining read.'
School Librarian

'Hilarious chaos!'
Books for Keeps